EBBTIDE 25 x 36 (91 x 63.4 mm.) 1985

Marjorie Tomchuk, 1989

M. Tomchuk

GRAPHIC WORK *1962-1989*

ACKNOWLEDGEMENTS

A special thank you to my husband, Howard and my son, Miles for their encouraging support during the planning and production of this book. The idea of creating this book is credited to Sylvia and Julian Olejniczak. They spent many hours gathering biographical information and they printed an earlier version of the catalog raisonne. I wish to thank Sophie Acheson who has spent many days during the past fourteen years as an assitant in my studio. The manuscript was written by Franz Geierhaas and the preface by Charles Lane; they took time out of their busy schedules to make a personal contribution to this book.

Many thanks to Dale Kimball, Barbara Bendici, Richard Kaplan and all the staff at Eastern Press for their cooperation during the printing of this book.

I wish to thank the many art dealers and the corporate and private art collectors who own art by M. Tomchuk. All these names cannot be listed but the interest and appreciation shown remains an important element in the motivation and creativity of this artist.

Marjorie Tomchuk

Library of Congress Catalog Card Number: 88-50984

Marjorie Tomchuk, 1933-
M. Tomchuk Graphic Work

1. Tomchuk, Marjorie 1933-
2. Graphic Work, Catalogue Raisonné
3. Original Prints, American
4. Artist/Printmaker, Contemporary, American
5. Biography
I Franz G. Geierhaas   II Title: M. Tomchuk Graphic Work
ISBN 0-9621400-0-7

1st Edition 1989
M. Tomchuk Fine Arts Publishing
44 Horton Lane, New Canaan, CT 06840

Printed in the United States of America

WATER IMPRESSION 24 x 18 (61 x 45.5 mm.) 1962

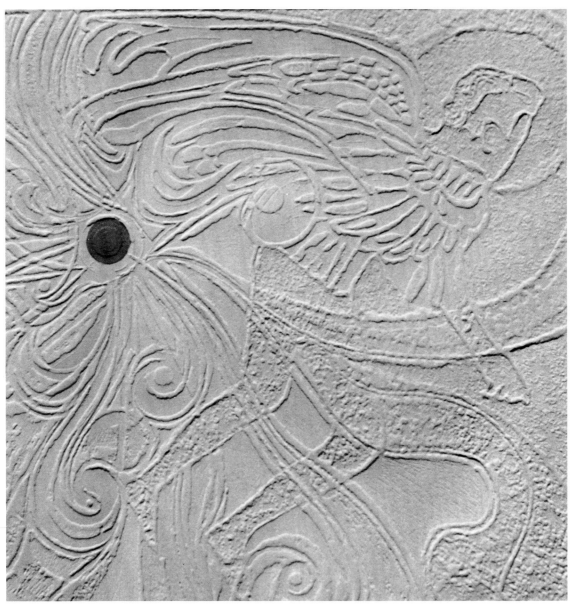

ICARUS 18 x 18 (46 x 46 mm.) 1969

CONTENTS

ECLIPSE I 36 x 26 (91 x 63.5 mm.) 1985

ECLIPSE II 36 x 26 (91 x 63.5 mm.) 1985

FRONDS 14 x 19 (35.5 x 48 mm.) 1987

PREFACE

Two very wide eyed people manned their first booth in the fall of 1979 at the Boston International Art Exposition and passed out copies of the *Journal of the Print World*; but however engrossed we were in learning about the world of art expositions, we did not fail to look at a poster and say, "Wow! That's excellent! Who did that?"

An artist named M. Tomchuk had done the poster; and as I purchased our first *Art Expo Poster*, I learned that M. Tomchuk was a lady. Other printmakers associated with the exposition had made posters, but we gave special attention to the booths of M. Tomchuk and Bernie Solomon. Within the year the *Journal of the Print World* had booths at the expositions in Washington, New York, and Chicago. M. Tomchuk had a booth at all except Chicago whose committee does not allow individual artists to take booths.

A few years have passed and we have now attended many expositions to find M. Tomchuk here and there. "Marjorie (as it turned out to be) apparently is doing well with those embossed etchings." We drew that conclusion as we knew the price for a booth at an art exposition. Marjorie Tomchuk has two. One has to be selling well to spend thousands of dollars up front before the show opens. We were happy about this as we very much liked the embossed etchings of Marjorie Tomchuk.

It is gratifying to learn that a printmaker is doing well at something she likes. At something original. At something distinctly hers. From the beginning in Boston in 1979 we had the feeling that no one else is doing this. No one else is using the medium quite this way and no one else is after the impact on the viewer that she is.

The intent of a work of art ought to be on the impact on the viewer that the artist genuinely wishes to share and is worth sharing. If the impact is pure emotion, it may be too personal or too childlike. If the impact is pure intellect, we may have reached abstract mathematics instead of a work of art. The first time that I looked at Marjorie's print of the Canadian *Wheatfields*, I felt the wheatfields and the wind. I did not need the title of the print nor anyone's explanation to help me.

The print has a powerful impact. It is intelligent and emotional. It is well dressed. It is soft spoken. It is well mannered. Look closely at all the prints. You can easily feel the very essence of each creation. The communication of the powerful impact is well-made. Very well-made as it is soft spoken, well mannered, well dressed. So is Marjorie Tomchuk.

In this book Franz Geierhaas explains how all this came about. In this brief preface, my goal is to tell you that you ought to be looking at these prints. Ask for her prints. Stop by her booth. Don't let this get away.

Charles Stuart Lane
Editor and Publisher
Journal of the Print World

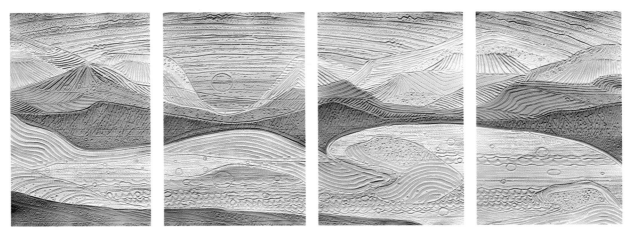

SIERRA 31 x 88 (79 x 224 mm.) 1980

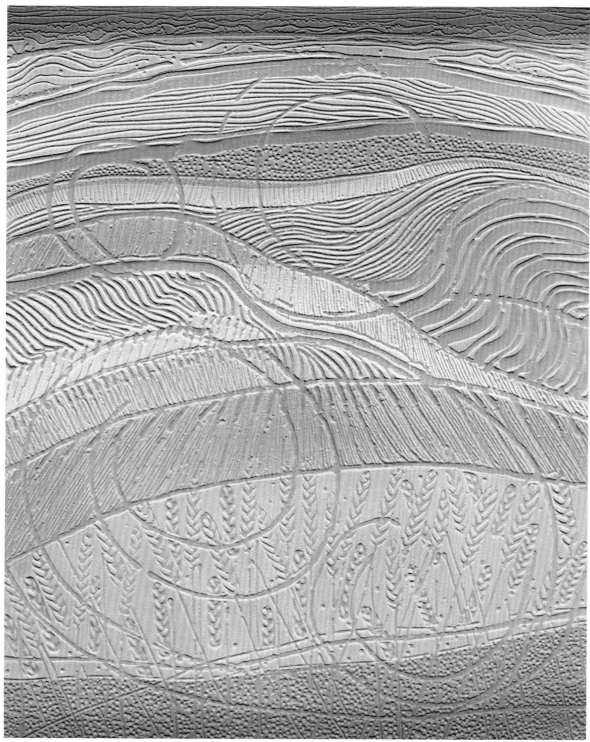

WHEATFIELDS 24 x 20 (61 x 51 mm.) 1979

RED EARTH 25 x 36 (63.5 x 91 mm.) 1985

THE ARTIST

Marjorie Tomchuk as an artist traversed a number of styles, techniques and images only to arrive as a masterful and mature creator where she began as a child. In her images of recent years she has incorporated the remembered spaces, colors, shapes and dynamics of her native Manitoba. This journey of hers is worth following in detail since it demonstrates the power of early shaping experiences of a person's way of perceiving, and ways of relating herself to the geographical as well as social and cultural environment, now integrated into strong images speaking of love of life expressed with extraordinary skill and technique. The artist's recent work has abandoned literary references and specific urban or geographical depiction in order to present us with almost Platonic ideas of what waves, mountains, winds, sun and clouds really are. If this reporter were a Jungian psychologist, he would insist that these are archetypical images. As the reader will shortly learn, wheatfields undulating in the winds, snow banks reminiscent of sand dunes, hoar frost patterns forming on windows and aurora borealis from endless summer skies are vividly remembered by Tomchuk, as are the tightly and densely organized patterns of Ukrainian folkart which were the only man-made art in young Marjorie's life. These patterns became the *embroidery* of the recent waves and spiral images. Anyone who has ever visited an artist's studio will remember the array of seemingly unrelated objects trouves on window sills or shelves which somehow find their way into the imagery later.

Recent psychological research has demonstrated that the human infant apperceives and interacts with his environment much earlier than had been previously thought possible and that preferential shapes, colors, sounds and smells are established very early indeed. The creative artist's path is rarely linear. It is usually characterized by detours, exploratory wandering, foreign exposure, educational and personal growth. This is true of Tomchuk's development, as well. The need to be accepted by peers, teachers and the art loving (and art buying) world is strong and many artists have succumbed to fashion and fad of the day. Tomchuk, an astute observer of the art scene for many years, recognized that accommodation is both, helpful and hampering. An extraordinary sense of integrity has kept her from falling prey to the demand of the facile and superficial and thus permitted her to continue in her search for her style and imagery which characterize her current work. It is only because she has freed herself from whatever dependency on dealer's advice and cajoling she had temporarily tolerated, that the stored and digested images of her early formative years have emerged.

Nature depicted "in the raw" is not art. Man's willfulness superimposes order and shape, in Tomchuk's case combined with distinctive elegance reflecting her own personality.

Marjorie Tomchuk was born in central Canada. Her parents were Ukrainians who had come over to become homesteaders in the vast flat reaches of Manitoba. Her paternal grandparents had immigrated to Canada as well and lived only a short walking distance away. Although Marjorie had one older brother and sister each, she really grew up very much alone. In a transcript of a taped interview with Julian M. Olejniczak, Marjorie

SUMMER BREEZE 14 x 19 (35.5 x 48 mm.) 1987

fondly recalls many of her childhood experiences. Reflecting no doubt on today's unsafe world, she reports on the feeling of safety and security she had throughout her childhood. Walking to school or her grandparent's farm, spending endless hours playing by herself outside the house happened with a child's curious eyes and trusting naivite.

The first farm which her father homesteaded was on an almost perfect circle of land about one-sixteenth mile in diameter surrounded by huge spruce trees and on a small hill. Marjorie played under these giant spruce trees every summer until she went to school. Much later she learned that the land had been owned and cultivated by Cree Indians, there were artifacts from an encampment and she believes that the spruce trees had been planted by the Crees as a windshield.

Marjorie was especially fond of her paternal grandparents - her mother's parents had remained in the Ukraine - she realizes now that they had about them a very East European peasant look. "My grandmother wore very long skirts, full of gathers at the top and reaching down to the ankles. I remember them as colorless but surely there must have been shades of blues and browns. The workshoes worn were very heavy. My grandmother tended a magnificent vegetable garden, curiously planted in the shape of a triangle. As a child I cherished her strawberries. Her garden was the same from year to year and was geometrically divided with paths and a formal plan."

Most of us expect an artist to have been surrounded by art or artists in childhood. Not so for Marjorie Tomchuk. The walls in the house might have sported "calendar art", but there were no art books available in her home or one-room school. The only artistic stimuli were Ukrainian folk art as depicted in the costumes worn during folk dance class and in the embroidery and crocheting pieces her mother made. She believes that her mother had innate talent because her Ukrainian Easter Eggs were the most elaborate and beautiful for miles around.

When Marjorie Tomchuk visited Russia in 1965 she had an experience of deja-vu while riding from the airport to the center of town. She realized that the houses along the road were very similar to her grandparents' house in Manitoba: low structures, windows decorated with carved frames; the panes were of double thickness, the side of the houses were protected by a foot-thick berm of soil and manure that had become compacted and was used as a primitive bench. Many Ukrainian houses were filled with pictures of all sizes with the apparent intent to cover every inch of space. This use of wall space was probably influential in Marjorie's own work later on when she developed very densely packed images in some of her woodcuts and etchings. "I grew up with what were patterns with a near-Eastern feeling. I remember having a Ukrainian folk dance costume which had a very busy cross-stitch decoration all over it; it seemed that the more decoration there was, the more beautiful the costume was considered. When I was about three years old, I remember that we had a small ornamental carpet made of cotton velour, about three by four feet at the most; I loved it because it was a mass of luxurious colors. One day much later I suddenly saw in the middle of the carpet a beautiful golden dog spread out like a magnificent sphinx, looking at me. This then became a truly magical carpet for me now that I was apparently mature enough to perceive the figure of the dog."

After one year in Winnipeg during Marjorie's first grade in school, the family moved back to Fisher Branch and lived in town where the girl attended a three-room school. Marjorie as a first grader learned both the English and Russian alphabets. She became fascinated by the different letters, some actual reversals in the two languages as regards the sounds associated with them. "Being exposed to another alphabet in the first grade was a profound learning experience for me and, although I did not fully understand the impact at the time, I do remember being pleasantly surprised that there were at least two different solutions to the creation of an alphabet." The artist insists that this early experience taught her a valuable lesson: various paths and solutions can be developed for any problem.

During fourth grade the family moved back to a farm which had already been homesteaded. The house was made of logs, it had two floors and from the second floor windows one had a magnificent view of the countryside all around.

The impact which these physical surroundings had on Marjorie as she grew up can best be reported in her own words. "I especially remember the summers during which I really had nothing to do except for some chores around the house such as dishwashing. I had a lot of time on my hands. One of the things I did was draw. I also made a lot of cut-outs. I remember taking the old Eaton's catalog (Canada's equivalent to the Sears' catalog) and had a wonderful time cutting out people and constructing a little village or stage setting. This was a very easy thing for me to do and to this day I sometimes work with cutouts and overlapping layers of color. I use layers of color and transparencies, one over the other. I find the cutout technique particularly helpful when I want to find out what shapes and colors I want to work with."

Although Marjorie Tomchuk did not emulate her mother as an embroiderer or Easter Egg painter, she feels that she did acquire her mother's almost "workaholic" attitude to life. "Her hands were never idle; she was always doing something. I do recall asking her why she did not just sit back and relax, yet I find myself becoming more and more like her. As my art career progresses, I find myself getting busier and busier, even though a year ago I could not conceive of getting any busier. There is something about creating art which is compulsive. Once you start you keep thinking of all the things you want to create as well as future projects you wish to tackle."

Most of all, Marjorie Tomchuk is convinced that the geographical and natural environment had an enormous impact on her. "The winters are what I remember most vividly. They were so very long and very cold. Temperatures commonly dipped down to 30 below zero, snowstorms lasted from two to three days; we would be completely covered in snowsuits with scarves over our faces so that only our eyes would show. And even then frost would form on our eyelashes causing them to stick together. I also vividly remember the snowbanks. On the plains the windblown snow would accumulate along treelines with daytime thaws resulting in thick crusts on the banks. Sometimes we could walk on these snowbanks all the way to school, at other times they would collapse and plunge us into snow waist deep. I also remember the sounds of winter. In the evenings

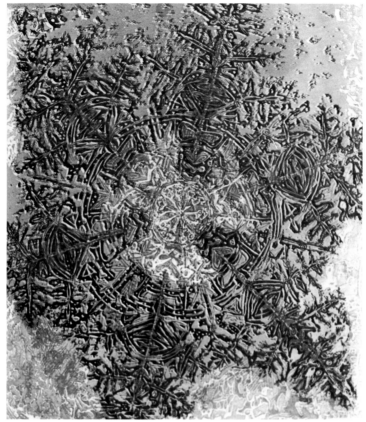

SNOW CRYSTAL 19½ x 17½ (49.5 x 44.5 mm.) 1976

the voices of people and the barking of dogs would carry extraordinary distances so that one could very clearly hear neighbors living two miles away. I also remember the great stillness of the winter nights and the walks in winter on clear nights with a full moon. This is the country where the horizon is not 180 but seems like 190 because there is so much sky. The land is very flat and thus you feel simply overpowered by the sky and the night stars. During winter with a full moon on the plains and the snow, it is a startling experience to have it appear so near daylight when in reality it is deep night.''

"I delighted in watching hoarfrost take shape on the windows. I would study the patterns for hours since no single pattern ever repeated itself. Sometimes I would breathe on the frost until it melted a circle several inches in diameter. I then sat watching the frost reform itself before my eyes like a white kaleidoscope.'' The magic of winter came to an end suddenly when snow and ice broke up and gave way to slush and mud. The crows' call heralded spring which was always welcome.''

Marjorie Tomchuk considers herself lucky not to have been sent to summer camp, of whose existence she did not even know at the time, but to be on the farm as the wheat her father grew ripened. In one of her perhaps most significant memories of that time she recalls, "I spent many hours looking out of the second floor window and observing the patterns of the fields. I watched the seasonal changes: in the spring it was the planting with very rich, black soil; gradually as the wheat grew, there were deep intense greens. For me the ripening wheatfields seemed to last forever. They changed from various shades of greenish-yellow to a lemon-yellow and then to a very rich, deep yellow culminating in almost yellow-ochre in the late summer. The wind had a tremendous effect on the wheatfields. I could see the currents of air as they moved along the fields from quite a great distance away until they were right near my house. These movements I watched for hours on end. I imagine children near the ocean watch the ocean waves just as I sat in the heart of Canada, far away from oceans and lakes, being fascinated by the wind making patterns in the living wheat."

Tomchuk recalls the crystal clear and extremely dry August days. When she asked her uncle, who still lives in Manitoba, whether her memories of the extraordinary display of Aurora Borealis or northern lights in the summer of 1949 were correct, he confirmed that none had been more spectacular since. "They seemed to come down in the sky very low. We children would yell at them and, after a few seconds, the lights would vibrate and move quickly which convinced us that they had reacted to our voices. The beauty of the northern lights, the intensity of colors as they flashed across the sky, or as they suddenly appeared and then just as suddenly disappeared, all this was a marvel and very mystical to me." It is certainly not too far-fetched to suggest that these memories are part of the motivational matrix behind Tomchuk's imagery today. One might even hypothesize that only now that she has become the fully assured master of technique and imagery is it possible for these very early and impressive experiences to reappear and find expression in her work.

When asked whether she does not miss the open spaces, the endless sky and the light that goes with them, the artist confesses that although she loves the verdancy of hilly Connecticut, she often yearns to see more sky. She has found that this wish could be fulfilled if she looked up from the parking lot of the nearby shopping center. This yearning still present now testifies to the internalization of early experiences. Another person who grew up in mountain valleys might have a similar yearning for those spaces if confronted with the vastness of the plains in the North American west.

It also appears that the lack of books which Tomchuk mentions several times in conversation had a contributing effect on her mature art. Children who read a lot incorporate into their fantasies many of the images suggested by the books. As they grow older the imagery will include farther and farther away places and events, thus covering up, as it were, some of the very early imagery. The fact that so many of Marjorie Tomchuk's recent prints present shapes, patterns, colors, and movements directly related to very early and sustained experiences throughout childhood may be ascribed to the absence of book-inspired fantasies and imagery. Although the artist decries her bookless childhood at one point, she may inadvertently have benefited from it in her recent work.

During the family's first residence in the city of Winnipeg, Marjorie remembers vividly her first experience of crossing a nearby bridge across the Red River. She was six at the time. Even today the artist has dreams about this bridge and the water flowing underneath it. "I remember standing on this structure made entirely of heavy metal beams with no wood planking anywhere and looking through the spaces between the metal grating at the rushing current below. Perhaps because I had no experience with rushing and large amounts of water before, I was frightened, hoping not to fall into

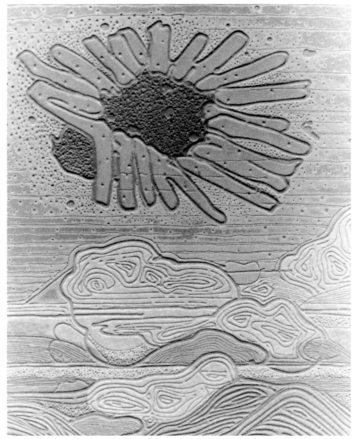

SUMMER SOLSTICE 24 x 20 (61 x 51 mm.) 1979

the rushing torrent, especially during the spring floods.'' Bridges have played a significant role in Tomchuk's imagery. The bridge span is for her both aesthetic form and psychological expression. Perhaps for a Freudian the manifest content of the dream just recalled suggests yet deeper layers, but artists are not only making manifest that which is hidden but usually make use of easily remembered images from the past as well.

What is always fascinating in artists' biographies is to learn when the future artist first came into contact with art and when she actually started to engage in artistic work. Marjorie Tomchuk as a child did a lot of drawing and made hundreds of paper cutouts. But so does almost every other child. Marjorie's earliest recollection of art was a snowman drawing she did in first grade for which she received high praise from the teacher. "The fact that the proportions were accurate, that the bottom circle was larger than the middle circle, and the top circle was the smallest, must have had some impact on my teacher. It seemed that I was very much in control of my circles at such a tender age."

The family moved back to Winnipeg when Marjorie was in eighth grade. The young girl often visited the landscaped grounds around the government buildings next to which was a multipurpose structure housing a rollerskating rink and the Natural History Museum which also had two or three rooms which housed the beginning of the Winnipeg Art Museum.

21

DARK AUTUMN 22½ x 17½ (52 x 44.5 mm.) 1963

It was only when Marjorie was in Junior High School that she went to this art section for the first time. "I remember standing for the longest time in the rooms which held the art collection wondering about the processes leading to the goal of having a painting on the walls of a museum. It was a revelation to me that someone, somewhere was creating artwork, the kind of artwork which a museum would hang for people to come to see and to admire. At that moment it would never have occurred to me that I would ever travel that route myself."

The Junior High School was located in a creaky old building, three stories high which had a silo-like fire escape whose metal spiral interior one could slide all the way down. The best fun was having a fire drill at Mulvy Junior High. On the serious side, it was at this school that Marjorie had different teachers for each subject including art and music. Art class met once a week and during spring and autumn the teacher would take the pupils outdoors to draw trees or the school building. They were also taught lettering which impressed the pupil who had just come from a one-room school where lettering did not receive high priorities. She enjoyed learning this new skill of drawing a very formal and precise letter one inch high with serifs. Perspective drawing was another skill acquired. "We also did watercolors and were introduced to the usual media taught at this level. It was a very broadening experience and one of my favorite classes - one that I had an easy time with. It took no effort at all to do well in art."

The High School Marjorie attended did not offer art classes and so - to her own surprise to this day - she, the usually reticent girl, became assertive enough to march to the principal's office and inquire about art classes. Another girl and she were subsequently permitted to go to another high school once a week for art instruction which she recalls as being excellent. In her own school she did the drawings for the yearbook, in a way a first art commission for her. She also won a competition prize of $5.00. "My entry in the competition was a surrealistic drawing. The influence of Dali's work was pervasive at the time. I did a watercolor on a 9″ x 12″ sheet. The shape of the main image was an hourglass with playing cards and hands coming out of it. The theme represented good and evil. I do not remember why I chose it. It was a lot of fun and winning the prize made me feel quite good, too. My mother kept that watercolor for a long time but it has now disappeared."

Like many a bright high school graduate then and now, Marjorie Tomchuk was not sure what was to come next. She toyed with a career in nursing but, perhaps because of her father's question as to whether she really believed that she actually wanted to become a nurse, she decided against it.

One of the key features of Marjorie's life up to then had been an enormous amount of freedom. She was never pressured into any plan of action. Her mother sympathetically advised her that whatever she chose to do she should do to the best of her ability. School work came easy or was non-existent. Time on her hands called for self-initiated action. The artist is now convinced that this freedom and ensuing responsibility for choosing a course of action by and for herself also became the exciting basis for her work in art. "What I am doing is something that I choose to do myself. This is a very important element of being an artist. You have no one telling you this should be done or that should be done. The choices are entirely your own. I believe this is true of life itself. If something goes wrong or if something goes right, you can only blame or praise yourself." Marjorie Tomchuk's *current* reflections on this freedom and the exhileration it engenders is certainly also due to her emergence as her *own* creative agent. Her work today is a highly personalized and unique expression of her vision of the world born out of her unique life experiences. This feeling of freedom which comes also from being the master of one's expressive means is the final reward for leaving behind all attempts at being "with it", i.e. being part of an artistic fashion or fad.

It was an opportunity for "time out." Marjorie got a job in a bank and quickly rose to the position of teller. She learned a lot about finance and accounting which stands her in good stead to this day in managing the business side of her art career. One lesson she learned remained vividly in her memory: "I remember that the bank manager would say to me as I struggled to balance the huge ledger sheets and came up a few cents off, 'no Marjorie, it's not the machine, it's you.' If he said it once he said it a half-dozen times. He ended up being correct. It is the input which is important, not the machine."

Restless after a year at the bank and with sufficient savings at hand, Marjorie decided to enroll in the School of Interior Design of the University of Manitoba. During her one year there, she benefited especially in the classes in mechanical drawing. To this day, Tomchuk uses these skills especially in designing her own ads for art magazines. Other classes she recalls were in fibers, materials, textiles, textures and, an especially good class, in colors using the color wheel, mixing colors and color compatibility.

In the summer of 1953 the family moved to Michigan where there were relatives and from where Marjorie's father and mother had originally gone to Manitoba.

Tomchuk immediately enrolled in the Art School of the University of Michigan in Ann Arbor. Only a few of her University of Manitoba credits were accepted as there was no degree program in interior design offered at Michigan. She changed her major to commercial and advertising art and learned a lot of skills in layout, et al. Alongside the commercial art courses she enrolled in courses in drawing and painting. She also took a course in printmaking. Due to the credit transfer and overload in her early years she was finished with her course requirements long before her residency requirements had been fulfilled. This enabled her to take some graduate art courses and courses leading to teaching certification. At that point Tomchuk had no desire or plan to teach. Her career goals were in the business world working for an advertising agency.

Most artists who have gone through art training at a university report ambivalent feelings about their educational experiences and teachers. So does Marjorie Tomchuk. Not only do her comments add to our understanding of her, the artist, but also provide food for thought on the entire range of problems on how to train an artist. One of her intents was to take courses in as many art media as possible. She did not specialize in any one field or medium, as a matter of fact, she now knows that she was a woman in search of a medium with which she would feel comfortable. "I found the printmaking class very enjoyable. It required a lot more discipline than any of the other classes. It was difficult to gain control of this medium so that I could predict more or less what the final product would be like. Perhaps it was the challenge posed by this medium

Tomchuk looked around for studio space and print workshops where she might take instruction or work. She enrolled in an etching class of Dick Swift's at Long Beach State College. The class became an eye-opener for her in several ways. She did not need the credits, she just wanted to develop further in her creative work and wanted to do what *she* wished.

Dick Swift believed in, and encouraged, experimentation. He believed that one should never abandon an etching plate, rather make it yield something else yet. He introduced Marjorie to color etching. Having studied with Stanley Hayter, he was familiar with that master's viscosity technique which allowed the simultaneous application of different colors on one plate. The freedom for experimentation and the knowledge and skills conveyed to the class made this one of Marjorie's most enjoyable and profitable learning experiences. She now had a bulging portfolio of prints created both, at the University of Michigan and at Long Beach State College, so that she could walk into galleries to show them to dealers some of whom were quite impressed and exhibited and sold some of her work. The young artist, needless to say, was pleased and reassured.

The following year Marjorie applied to teach at an American Dependent School in Japan and luckily was assigned to a school in central Tokyo. It was located near the Meiji Shrine with its superb gardens. One of Tomchuk's first impressions of Japanese methods came while observing many people meticulously maintaining and manicuring this park by hand.

Japan for Marjorie Tomchuk as for uncounted others who visited or lived there was a source of continuous wonder and revelation. She admired not only the very different buildings, gardens, tools and natural scenery, she was also captivated by the *different ways* the Japanese tackled daily living and work.

She avidly absorbed the aesthetic as well as historical/symbolic lessons of such varied places as the garishly decorated shrines in Nikko, and the pristine simplicity of the Shrines in Ise, which mysteriously occupy the shady ground below tall pine trees. She sat in awe across from the stone garden at Ryoanji Temple in Kyoto and absorbed the Shinto lesson of the spirituality of things when she saw the "married rocks" in the water near the beach. A large rock and a smaller rock are united by a rope embracing both of them.

It was in Japan that Tomchuk finally came into her own as a printmaker. It was here that she decided that printmaking was the most satisfying of all the media she had tried. Never having forgotten her business skills, she also recognized that prints were more marketable than were oils. They were also more readily moved and shipped. This decision to concentrate her talents on printmaking was aided by her experiences with two Japanese teachers.

She took a course in Japanese woodblock technique with Toshi Yoshida. His father, Hiroshi Yoshida, a well known woodcut artist, had studied European techniques during those decades after the Meiji Restoration when European artistic styles such as Impressionism became the rage in Japan. Hiroshi taught both his sons who became very well known artists themselves. Toshi spoke English well enough to give lessons to Gaijins (foreigners). "What I most looked forward to on weekends was going to the

Yoshida house for lessons. At first, everything was very strange - the train ride, finding his house in a maze of unmarked streets and alleyways; the strange tools and his instructional philosophy. On Saturdays he had about five students. His house was always open. I was most fascinated by the tools and materials he used and taught us to use. A sharkskin stretched on a board served as a sander. Totally new to me, this tool had been in use in Japan for centuries and represents probably the best sander imaginable. Bamboo leaves stretched over a flat pad of tough rope serving as a baren with which one pressed the paper onto the inked woodblock. All tools used were made out of natural materials: no plastic, nothing synthetic, very little metal except for cutting tools." Marjorie learned to use the very straight cutting tools the Japanese prefer to the curved ones customary in the West. When today she has to gouge any wood surface she takes out her Japanese tools. They are more effective, easier to grasp and simply work better for her. In his instruction Yoshida did not insist on a specific style. He simply provided all information on the Japanese technique for cutting woodblocks, and choosing the best wood for a specific style. Yoshida prefers waterbased inks. He taught his student how to grind chunks of pigment in a mortar with a pestle before adding rice-based glue and water to make the ink. It is necessary to keep the wood wet like a sponge and apply the ink to the surface with a large thick brush. The wood absorbs the ink and holds it so that when the dampened paper is applied, both surfaces are damp and everything meshes together in the final impression. Yoshida also taught Marjorie the technique of blending a number of colors together on a single, very wide brush. This brush, which could be as large as six inches across, could have blue on the top, green in the middle and yellow on the bottom. By carefully applying it to the woodblock, one could create a wonderful band of blended gradations of colors.

The second teacher Tomchuk had in Japan was Uchiyama who taught Sumi-e, i.e. ink brush painting. Various sized brushes are applied with sumi on thin Japanese paper (often erroneously called *rice* paper. Japanese paper is usually made from the inside of the bark of the mulberry tree). "I specifically recall an exercise involving irises. Irises are one of two flowering plants found in formal Japanese gardens. The other is azalea. Uchiyama had a vase of irises in front of him and he had blooms scattered naturally on the floor. He sat on the floor on a tatami mat and spread his white paper before him on another mat. We, in turn, sat on the floor in front of him and watched him. He carefully explained to us both how and why he did what he did. First he would take a very wide, round brush, dip into water and then into a thinner mixture of sumi to produce a light grey. Next he put the tip of the brush into black, very intense sumi. With one stroke he was able to achieve a beautiful gradation of shades from white through light grey to dark to black. With his incredible control he was able to create an almost photographic image of the iris. Though intensely controlled, it radiated spontaneous creativity and naturalness."

Tomchuk bought a car which permitted her to drive out into the Japanese countryside. With her newly acquired 35mm camera, she began to take stock of what intrigued her about Japan. One memorable trip was to the pottery village of Mashiko. Japanese pottery traditionally is made near the best available clay. Entire villages sprang up consisting entirely of potters and their families. Mashiko is one of these where very creative pottery is produced to this day. Tomchuk was fascinated by the long kilns built tunnel-like into the hillside. In the village each hut had a porch with a protruding eave over it. On the porch, the owner's pottery was displayed for sale. She filled her car with pottery and took it back to Tokyo. The fact that these potters started from scratch, i.e. making their own clay, and completed their pots in hand-built kilns impressed Tomchuk immensely. It represented a philosophy of creativity which she herself began to embrace. It certainly is represented in her work involving handmade paper and handcast plates. Embracing this attitude towards creating shows both, a desire for total control and an ability upon completion of the work, to be able to say I made this, all of it.

In the school where she taught, she had a number of Japanese or partly Japanese students, she learned yet another important lesson: Culturally conditioned methods of doing things are not easily transferable to another culture. One episode will illustrate this experience of hers: "Little things drew my attention, for instance how the Japanese drew an arrow. My arrows always had two barbs, top and bottom. They drew an arrow with a straight line and a single barb on top. The first time I saw a Japanese child draw one, I had to ask him what it was. I then corrected him by adding a second barb. Being Japanese he was very polite and said nothing. Several days later I noticed a number of arrows around the town drawn this way: straight line, one barb." Tomchuk realized again that there is more than one way of achieving the same goal. "Personal lessons like the one with the arrow were invaluable for me because they made me realize that my Western background needed to be broadened to accept a whole new culture and to accept other approaches to the interpretation of the world around us." This insight validates anew a major statement by anthropologist Ruth Benedict who in the introductory sentences to her classic "Patterns of Culture" wrote: "No man ever looks at the world with pristine eyes; rather he sees it edited by the patterns of his culture." If we wish to understand another culture we must understand the frame of reference within which members of that culture operate.

Tomchuk made two extensive trips to India from Japan during her summer breaks. She and her traveling companion, Mary Lou Manor, also visited Sri Lanka, Cambodia, Nepal, and Vietnam. The experiences were intense especially since they traveled on local trains and buses and got to see and feel the way people really lived, worked, and celebrated various rites of passage. They were curious and disappointed that they found no contemporary art reflecting these cultures. Most contemporary artists were adapting Western styles, such as abstract expressionism, and Western imagery.

The two-year stay in Japan and these extensive trips became the source of imagery for many of Tomchuk's prints, a discussion of which will follow.

Tomchuk's next station was Frankfurt, Germany where she taught for a year. She was fortunate to meet Helga Kaiser, a superb printmaker, and was able to work in her studio. During this year, still under the spell of the Far East, Tomchuk created a series of small-scaled etchings experimenting with all sorts of intaglio techniques. She transferred her color print experience with Japanese-style woodcuts to etching. Helga

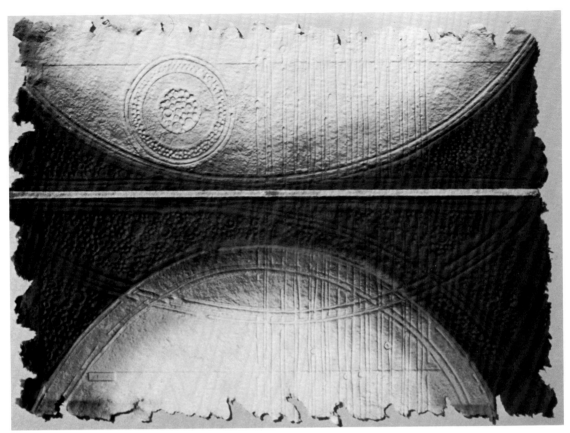

SPAN 25 x 36 (63.5 x 91 mm.) 1984

Kaiser was most helpful to her as regards sources for necessary materials. Often Kaiser had them available in her spacious studio.

In the summer of 1965, Tomchuk moved back to the United States and settled in New York City. She found a small apartment and went to Pratt Graphics Center to work in printmaking. Surrounded by other printmakers, students as well as established artists, Tomchuk felt strongly influenced by what was going on around her. "I felt that if I was in New York working at printmaking I had to live up to some kind of artistic standard. Here I was, all of a sudden in the center of the art world and doing my own thing, experimenting, not really giving a hoot what my images looked like, but doing what I wanted to do. I felt that that was not considered okay. Unfortunately, I think that many artists in New York fall into this trap. They are surrounded by what the galleries are showing, they read what the critics write and get to know what is the "in" thing. The newcomer will, unconsciously probably, begin to feel that his or her artwork has no validity unless it is in the acceptable or 'in' style in New York." Marjorie Tomchuk, at this time, was also employed as an art teacher in suburban Spring Valley, N.Y.

In 1966 she moved to a storefront with a studio apartment in back on McDougall Street in downtown Manhattan. At that time it was just a comfortable Italian neighborhood, very safe, very close. It might just as well have been Naples because of the clotheslines strung between the buildings, and with neighbors at the windows of the five storey building carrying on vociferous conversations in Italian. "At that time I purchased an etching press. When the press was installed, one of the Brand brothers

THE BRIDGE 19½ x 17½ (49.5 x 44.5 mm.) 1976

MEMORIAL TO AN ERA 20 x 16 (51 x 40.5 mm.) 1973

came along to supervise. As he left my studio, he wished me luck in my career as a printmaker. The purchase of this press actually signalled a change taking place in my life. I was now a very committed artist-printer."

Many lessons still lay ahead. One kind had to do with how to sell original prints. Tomchuk made contact with some print publishers. John Barton, an artist himself, was the first to buy some of her work. He gathered work from other artists to sell to galleries, department stores, interior designers and others. Tomchuk also sold to another publisher at this early stage of her professional career. This person saw some of her prints in the storefront window, knocked and came in. He bought forty impressions of *The Arabian Horse* for $7.50 each. Tomchuk learned that they were seen selling for $125 each on Long Island. "This kind of experience really shocked me. It was an important learning experience for me. This is what happens when you sell in odd lots to distributors of questionable reputation. It is standard practice that artists selling prints receive 20% or sometimes less of the final selling price."

Tomchuk also found that New York is a 'consignment' town. Most galleries will not buy prints or other art works outright but take them on consignment. Unless the gallery is enthusiastic about the artist's work, it often sits in bins or worse, lies hidden in the drawers. Collecting from these galleries for work sold is often very difficult.

At the time Tomchuk began working in New York, there were relatively few publishers of prints. A publisher commissions the artist to do editions for him with the artist only retaining a small number of Artist's Proofs (AP's) for her own use. The publisher pays the artist upon receipt of the edition and then distributes the edition through his salesmen and contact galleries. The artist, in other words, need not spend valuable time on seeking to distribute her own work. As indicated above, the publishers usually pay 1/5 or less of the retail price to the artist. Work sold on consignment usually brings 50% - if you get paid. The two most well known print publishers in New York in the mid-sixties were Sylvan Cole, Director of *Associated American Artists* and Abe Lublin of *Lublin Graphics*. Both of these men and their organizations were and still are among the most respected and ethical publishers and distributors of graphic art in the business, even though Sylvan Cole and Abe Lublin have left or retired from their respective companies. Associated American Artists takes prints on consignment whereas Lublin Graphics buys entire editions, in addition to keeping work on consignment.

Tomchuk's association with Lublin Graphics began in 1968. In her association with Abe Lublin and his company, she learned a number of valuable lessons from the experienced print dealer. Her told her, "make your prints easy to do. If you are working too hard at them, if you are trying too hard to create, they are not as good as when they come easy." At first she did not understand what Lublin meant. Once, however, when she showed him a print and he liked it, she said to him that it had been an easy one, he responded, "Great, that is terrific!" Later Tomchuk realized what he was trying to convey to her. "When creating a print comes easily and very naturally it is much more 'you'. It is a truly natural creation, it is not forced, it is not stiff. It is just a general flow from you to the medium in which you are working." Lublin also taught Marjorie only to sell her best work. Within an edition an artist might become careless, smudge the edge of the paper or overwipe the plate so the print becomes too light or, conversely, too dark, due to insufficient wiping. Perhaps he or she feels that two or three imperfectly done prints among a hundred do not matter. Lublin stressed to her that even if an artist delivers a carload of artwork, every print becomes a very individual piece to the person who ultimately purchases it to display in his home. Lublin helped Tomchuk not to get discouraged if not every one of her prints turned out a masterpiece. A really good dealer can help the artist develop a sense of critical self-appraisal of her work by pointing out to her which of the works presented to him are superior and which are not up to snuff.

Tomchuk also learned over the two decades of independent printmaking that sometimes when inspiration lagged or the colors just do not seem right, it may help to put the plate away for a while and come back to it later when the problem encountered earlier often disappears as if by itself.

In 1970, Marjorie Tomchuk became Mrs. Aronson. The couple moved to Connecticut a year later. Shortly thereafter Marjorie felt that the time had come to sever her relationship to Lublin Graphics. She felt that she had done all of the realistically and tightly drawn Americana prints she really wanted to do. She was ready to develop a new style which she felt had already begun to surface in some of her prints by that time. Tomchuk was not sure whether the new style would be successful and she also knew that Lublin preferred the realistic images she had created up to then. When she did leave Lublin, she could not just seek out another publisher. There were very few to begin with and they usually did not like to take on their competitor-friends' former artists. She now felt all alone. Beside the search for a new image and style, there was a wonderful new addition to her life. "My son, Miles, appeared on the scene and I was able to spend more time with him without being committed to doing artwork. My husband was, of course, very supportive of everything I did, yet he was very surprised when I began creating some new images so totally unlike any I had been doing before. I could not quite explain this to him, except to say that I wanted to do something different. He could not understand why because my other prints had always been very attractive to him. I just knew, his puzzlement notwithstanding, that I had to make a fresh start and most of all had to listen to my feelings."

Instead of looking for other publishers or galleries which would carry her work, Marjorie decided to market her artwork herself, primarily through two connected methods: advertising her showings at open art dealer conventions, or Art Expos, and by attending these Expos to sell. Very few individual artists have so consistently and successfully done as has Marjorie Tomchuk. The benefits of this approach are many, most of all, she, the artist keeps control of prices and except for the considerable cost of attending these Expos, she keeps all the income. The expenditure is much less than opening one's own gallery at some prestigious and expensive place. The artist, between Expos, can concentrate on her work and need not spend too much valuable time with the business end of the creative output.

Creating successful images and developing new processes invites imitators. Frequent thefts of ideas and techniques happen. At the Art Expo it becomes quickly apparent

VIEW FROM THE FERRY 24 x 18 (61 x 46 mm.) 1976

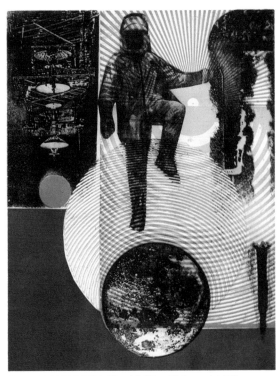

ONE GIANT LEAP 20 x 16 (51 x 40.4 mm.) 1970

VIEUX CARRÉ 20 x 16 (51 x 40.5 mm.) 1974

GRAND VICTORIAN 24 x 18 (61 x 46 mm.) 1975

who does a particular style or image first, and who, the following year are the copiers and imitators. And yet, open shows provide the opportunity for the essential artist-dealer-collector dialogue. "It is very exciting and stimulating to talk to the people who are buying your artwork. I thoroughly enjoy it and it is one of the aspects of being an artist that I look forward to." Tomchuk's advice to artists who are newcomers to the Art-Expo scene is to make sure their work retains a consistency of style and imagery over a number of years, the time it takes to be noticed and sink into the viewers' mind. It takes a long time to mature, and it takes a long time for a consistent body of work to appear. If artists believe in their own work, they should not give up on it. They should keep working at it year after year. These convictions of Marjorie Tomchuk's are lived by her in her approach to creating, exhibiting, and selling her prints.

THE PRINTS

Marjorie Tomchuk in her career as printmaker has used essentially three major techniques: woodcut, etching and the embossed color print. Each of these methods is described in the technique section. Readers familiar with these techniques will recognize that Tomchuk like every other artist developed her own personal 'gimmicks' to add to standard techniques. Combinations such as etching and embossment, or background cardboard color plates and embossed plates are common and are indicated in the catalog raisonné. Tomchuk's ideas and inspirations come from the environment in which she lives, from her many foreign residences and travels and from the hundreds of black and white photographs she took along the way. Quite often, impressions collected lie dormant as if being digested before coming to the fore months or years later for processing into a work of art. In Japan, major influences on Tomchuk were nature as arranged by man in planted as well as stone gardens, patterns produced on kimono cloth with stencils, exacting standards of perfection and increasingly a search for essence. This latter Zen-inspired-concept took hold of Tomchuk slowly and finds expression most poignantly in her recent work which has abandoned literalness and realism to be replaced by general statements on nature's shapes, formations and dynamics such as mountains, oceans, stars, the sun and the enormous movements and powers immanent in nature.

The path Tomchuk chose was guided by the need to be *au courant* as in her New York years, to produce saleable prints for her publisher, but perhaps even more and in the end triumphantly, by a search for *her* style and her means of expression which we see in her work of the last decade.

The following will be a brief summary of this development with significant examples cited which indicate turning points. They will be highlighted both as to concept, content and technique.

Any viewer of Tomchuk's work will be impressed by the technical excellence of execution as well as the originality of ideas and composition.

Some viewers may find her new prints of the last decade, when contrasted with her earlier styles, a total break and thus eliminating any claim for an organic development. The explanations below might help the reader to overcome this misleading impression.

In addition, there is plenty of precedent for stylistic turnabouts. We need only remember Picasso and Mondrian.

In her current work Tomchuk does not rely on her archive of photographs any longer, she now mines her memory and experience for the less specific and more abstract images.

In general, she starts with a series of quick line sketches, sometimes as many as twenty, to develop the image and its basic composition. When working on the plates, changes occur to amend the sketched image. When the plate has been developed to a certain point, a first proof print is made which initiates further changes and so on through sometimes a dozen proofs before the artist says to herself, 'bon a tirer,' the plate is now ready for printing the edition. Some of the most time-consuming plates though presaging further development such as *Ceremonials* are never editioned.

Tomchuk who often now works on three to six plates simultaneously requires absolute quiet to concentrate. She works mainly in the morning hours while fresh. Her assistant, Sophie Acheson, who has worked for her over a period of fourteen years, now makes the handmade paper which Tomchuk has used exclusively since 1984. Marjorie's son, Miles, also helps her from time to time.

In the woodcuts and etchings traditionally the chief image or configuration was printed in black, other blocks or plates were used to produce background color or overlapping minor images. Tomchuk, like collograph artists, often used a cardboard plate which she inked to produce background color. When she began using her deliberately coarse and pebbly handmade paper and tried to print these background colors she found that the rough surface would not accept the oilbased inks. When she ran plate and paper through the press a second time she found that the handmade paper had been flattened and its very characteristic surface textures had been destroyed. She stopped printing color through the press and started to use an airbrush, her method to this day. The plate created out of an industrial plastic is used for the embossment into the handmade paper with color application by airbrush second. Usually eighteen to twenty prints are made at one time and Tomchuk's decades of experience guarantee that they come out extremely close in colors. She now uses waterbased inks which have the further advantage, already mentioned, of keeping her allergies to petrochemical material at bay.

In Japan, Marjorie Tomchuk made only woodcuts. One of the first was entitled *Dark Autumn*. It was a study of tree shapes. She had been very much impressed by bonsai trees and often wondered whether not all the trees in Tokyo were trained by man's hands. Having arrived in Japan in late August, she felt the need to include in this print some of the fall colors encountered. She used shades of brown, grey, dull violet and blue. She also felt that she was at variance with Yoshida's woodcut techniques. In Michigan she had been taught - and this was the German Expressionist tradition - that the print must show some of the gouge marks made into the woodblock. It conveyed some of the energy needed to cut away at the block. For the Japanese such marks of tools used were of no importance or consequence. Tomchuk, however, retained them in her work. This print and others she created in Japan were primarily concerned with shapes and colors, overlapping colors, that is, which could produce either a muddy impression or,

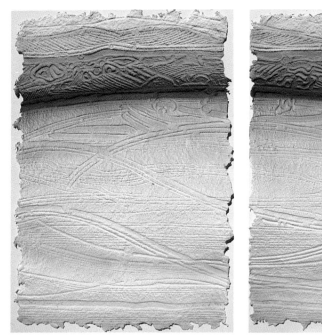

SEAWAY I & II 36 x 50 (91 x 127 mm.) 1986

if successful, some very pleasurable transparencies.

Some of the images produced in Japan arose out of the memory bank from travels to India and Cambodia. Among these, *Shiva* and *Angkor* stand out. In *Shiva* the artist for the first time used a gold metal in her waterbased ink on wood. She went through a whole series of trials before she achieved the effect of a glistening, golden Shiva. "The imagery was important because I wanted to capture the impact of the hundreds of such figures I had seen in India, but the real challenge became the use of the metallic paint."

Everyone who has been to Angkor in the jungles of northwestern Cambodia comes away awed by the series of huge and magnificently decorated temples, gates and other structures. So did Tomchuk. "As an artist it is difficult not to feel that it is more than a temple complex, the Angkor ruins are a most important monument of the creative genius of mankind in architecture. When I returned to Japan I had to attempt to capture some of the feeling of the greatness of the place, such as the huge heads over the entrance gates to Angkor Tom."

While in Frankfurt, working at Helga Kaiser's studio, Tomchuk created a series of small-scaled (12″ x 12″) etchings. It is interesting that the impact her two years in Asia had made on the artist, lingered on during her Frankfurt period and the imagery in the etchings reflects Asian themes. One of them, entitled *Buddha*, became a deep, dark grey, almost mystical print. Upon reflection now, the artist believes that she wanted to recreate her feelings of coming upon a Buddha statue in some dark temple interior. While in Helga Kaiser's studio, Tomchuk also enjoyed experimenting with intaglio techniques she had learned in Long Beach, California, three years before. Two of these experimental prints are *Indian Woman* and *Taj Mahal*. While the *Indian Woman* was done in deep ochre, sienna red, dark brown, and a suggestion of blue for the sky, *Taj Mahal* turned out very pale, pearlescent almost, because of the artist's use of pinks, light blues and light greys. "That to me *is* the Taj Mahal. It is another place which remains vividly in my memory even after a passage of many years. It is much more than a spectacularly beautiful building, it is a work of absolute art. So I did a print of Taj

GLACIAL PEAK 24 x 20 (61 x 51 mm.) 1983

OCEAN 24 x 20 (61 x 51 mm.) 1979

Mahal while in Germany because the experience was then still very much with me."

Only towards the end of her year there, did the artist create some European images. She remembers how comfortable she felt with producing a series of same-sized images. She felt relieved not to have to rethink the technical problems posed by each different-sized plate. Another advantage was the easy transportability of such small prints when she decided to return to the United States in the spring of 1965. One of the European images is called *Rose Window*. Tomchuk remembers her visits to the dark interiors of European cathedrals with the only light and color coming from the windows. Always fascinated by circles, she was particularly attracted to the rose windows which adorn French cathedrals. The print *Houses* reflects the gabled roofs and cobblestoned streets of medieval German towns.

Upon her return to the United States and before she could buy her own printing press, the artist worked on etchings while attending workshops at Pratt Graphics Center. She felt considerably confused at first: "What should the image be? Could it be 'me' or must it be a New York inspired image? My first New York etchings still retained some oriental feeling." There were two in particular: *Concentric Design* and *Chinese Modern*. The latter was also the first print in which Tomchuk used some embossing which has become the central technique in more recent prints. The simplicity of the composition of *Chinese Modern* is not only an hommage to Zen-inspired essential shapes, it is also a harbinger of compositional ideas to come. The etching entitled Solo once more embraces Japanese imagery but also shows some of the boldness of imagery then in vogue in New York (Franz Kline, et al.).

No one living in New York can ignore the masses of people, the density of cohabitation, often on top of one another. This impacted on Tomchuk as well. Many of her early New York prints contain a lot of human figures such as *Flight, The City, Sunday in the Park*, and perhaps most impressively, *Ave.A.B.C.D.* It remains a favorite

PACIFIC STORM I & II 31 x 44 (79 x 112 mm.) 1980

of the artist. "It is rather geometric in shape, and it has the busy-ness of the people and the streets. I had frequently driven past Avenues A,B,C, and D off Houston Street and, having recently returned from the Far East, I was impressed, perhaps even depressed by what I saw. There were endless rows of dwellings which looked like Federal Housing Projects with multitudes of people coming out of them. The existence of these multitudes disturbed me but the print turned into a very pleasant semi-abstract impression of this experience."

A few more woodblock prints in the Japanese manner followed, among them *Sunflowers* (a second version was done in 1969). Tomchuk had always loved sunflowers and whenever she encountered them, especially whole fields of them, she rejoiced in the experience. A 1979 embossed color print entitled *Summer Solstice* again picks up the sunflower theme. Once she found a piece of very old plywood board on Jones Beach. Sand and water had worn away the softer wood and left a woodgrain surface that had much strength. "I brought it back to my studio. This chance event led me to using its incredibly beautiful wood texture in a woodcut print. It was natural beauty which needed no chiseling or carving away. I incorporated it into a print using some of the woodcuts I had done in Japan. The silhouette tree pattern I had used before surfaced here again. I called it *Spring Approaches Visibly*."

Slowly, especially after the artist was successful in selling some of her prints and editions, she gained enough confidence to defy the pressure to be 'with it'. She began embossings for which she etched zinc, copper and brass plates very deeply. "I felt the resulting series of heavily embossed prints were really me, only me. This was probably the first time that I felt entirely comfortable with what I was doing in etching. The only other time when I had that feeling of total satisfaction was with my Japanese-style woodblock prints." The print Icarus shows a color-neutral background with deep embossing. Only one dot of orange, for the sun, is in the upper left. For the artist the

43

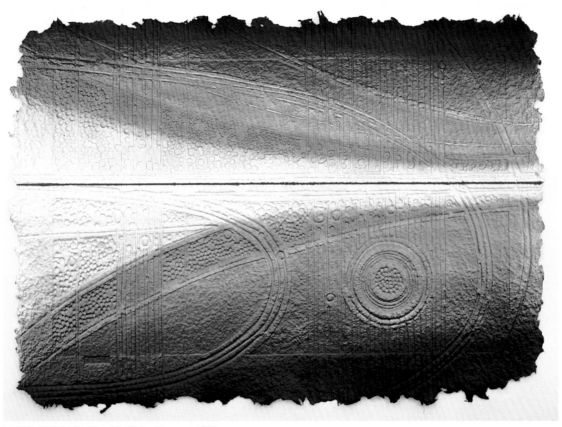

SONIC STREAM 25 x 36 (63.5 x 91 mm.) 1984

crucial dimension of this print is the total embossing. There followed a whole series of such deeply embossed prints, among them *The Phoenix, The Dancers* and *Abracadabra.*

In 1970 while still in New York, the artist had the idea to create a whole series of prints for a portfolio. She entitled the series *Americana* with each print bearing its own title as well and her goal was to use and master photo collage and photo montage on etching plates. At that time photo etching had not taken hold yet. There were no courses offered in it. Tomchuk experimented, asked for advice and did a lot of library research. "This series of ten Americana prints are not my usual embossed etchings. They are a group of work unique unto itself. Some of the ten prints have embossing in them but they relate primarily to a feeling I wanted to express about some of the important things happening in the United States. Seven of them were completed. They had such titles as *One Giant Leap* (a year before the Space Age had leapt forward with the American Moon Landings), *Freedom, Midwest Gothic, Urban Maze* (New York City), *Declaration, Melting Pot,* and *Frontier.* I felt very good about them; they were distinctly different." Some of the prints won prizes and one entered the collection of the National Air and Space Museum of the Smithsonian Institution.

Tomchuk did not continue with photo-etching beyond this series. A little later she began another Americana series which reflected mainly her travels with her husband in the United States. With her camera ever ready, with her own darkroom to develop,

RED PLANET 25 x 36 (63.5 x 91 mm.) 1988

crop and select her best images which, in her mind, would make good prints, there emerged a group of graphics which is altogether a joyful celebration of many places, events and people of the United States. *The Peanut Cart on Larimer Square* represents an actual such cart encountered in Denver. *From Another Era* is a composite of several images which she saw and photographed. So is *Old Number Three,* the locomotive; *Vieux Carré* in New Orleans, *Apothecary* and musicians on *Ghirardelli Square.* A particularly strong image is *View from the Ferry* which catches the imposing skyscrapers of Lower Manhattan. The print *Grand Victorian* literally overwhelms the viewer with its gables and towerlets. As these images were created the artist, always eager to try something new, developed some ideas, actually in part a fall-back to her oriental experiences, which found expression in the print *The Bridge.* The feeling of a flowing composition, the bridge and its reflection in the water carefully balanced add up to a contemporary statement which was absent in the earlier prints. *Icarus* and an embossed etching of 1970, *Northern Landscape* are like trial balloons on the way to new imagery, style and statement. "Perhaps I denied to myself that those prints were the ones to follow because of the New York pressures. For a while I strayed from my artistic path. All of these things and pressures pull at an artist's mind, and now I reaiize that none of them is the least bit important. But at that time when I should have been occupied with developing *my* style, I did not realize that prints such as *Icarus, The Bridge,* and *Northern Landscape* were actually clues as to what direction I should take. They were prints which came easily, they were prints which were successful and, they did not look

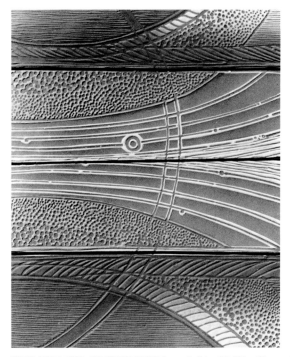

COSMIC RAYS, COSMIC SWIRL each 24 x 20 (61 x 51 mm.) 1983

like anyone else's. But I was not astute enough at that point in time to pick up on that; I think this is part of the maturing process each artist has to go through."

Besides the three forward-looking prints mentioned, there were others which carried the germ of things to come. They included *Homage to Van Gogh, Snow Crystal,* and perhaps most of all, the *Silvermine Guild Poster* of 1972. The artist even used the same masterplate as in *Northern Landscape* in creating this poster.

Trails End, perhaps prophetically named, was one of the last tightly drawn images based on photographs. There follows a lightening of the composition after a trip to the Southwest. American Indian motives appear, among them *Cermonial, On the Plains, Shield, Indian Girl,* and *Bison.* Tomchuk draws attention to the circular flowing movement of lines in *Shield* as another overture to her recent imagery.

During the year 1976 Marjorie Tomchuk, who had not sold a lot of work even though she had some shows and placed her work with dealers, decided that she should try to exhibit at the up-and-coming art fairs beginning with WASH ART. It turned out that this was a good decision and since then most of her showings and sales are at or connected with art fairs all over the world.

By 1978, the artist felt an urgent need to change her style. She had been working with metal plates for a number of years. Her images were realistic, tightly drawn and representational as in the two *Americana* series. As often happens, a serendipitous encounter opened the way to new experimentation with color. A Canadian woman visited Tomchuk in her studio one day and, after studying the etchings shown to her, she asked the artist, "Why are all of them so dark and so black?" Tomchuk explained to her that this was not so much by choice but was inherent in the nature of prints made from metal plates. Etching on metal plates meant using black ink for the main image. "Yes, but black is so depressing", retorted the visitor. Tomchuk who had never thought that the black line etchings would have a depressing impact on some viewers decided to begin experimenting with brighter colors with the aim of abandoning the

MARQUEE 25 x 36 (63.5 x 91 mm.) 1988

black-lined images altogether. Two goals demanded her attention simultaneously: The search for black-free, lighter-colored images and a departure from the realism of her prints so far. The print, entitled *Ocean* represents a breakthrough in these directions. This embossed print was still colored by means of plates run through the press. The break was not complete. There was still some black etching ink in the image but it was no longer the dominant feature. It took her another year before she dropped the use of black ink altogether. *Eventide* became the major breakthrough print. "I used my new technique of forming a heavily embossed plate from industrial plastic. The background colors were hand-rolled, the color of the print was run through the etching press, and the embossing was put on last. My style was very "loose", with free flowing lines. The work went very smoothly and with hardly an effort. I was very comfortable with the entire procedure and continued to make prints in this style. They drew a lot of attention from viewers, many of whom commented on the 'peacefulness' of the subject matter."

Soon after entering this new stylistic phase, Tomchuk came full circle in expressing deep-seated memories of early childhood experiences. *Wheatfields* is the first of these embossed color prints. She had always been partial to the changing yellows and the dynamics of the windblown fields of wheat all around her family's farm. This print became an affirmation of her very *own* root values free of acquired temporary adaptations to prevalent styles dictated by the New York art world. These prints were very well received at the Washington and New York art fairs thus giving her additional confirmation that she was on the right track. The diptych *Pacific Storm* was her first

STELLAR GATE 25 x 36 (63.5 x 91 mm.) 1985

double print - many multiprint works were to follow later such as *Sierra* - in which she felt that no longer did she have to contain her image within etching plate sizes of 16″ x 20″ or, at most 18″ x 24″. Her new plates weighed much less, they could be larger and provided her with an opportunity to share with her viewers the immensity of her early experiences and give expression to her yearning for the wide-open spaces and towering skies. Many of her images still were inspired by journeys with her family but she relied less and less on her camera. A trip to Yosemite yielded the print called *Canyon, any* canyon or, *the* canyon. There was no longer any literal reference in her work. These recognizable landscape prints soon gave way to ever more abstract treatment of the world around her. "In the prints titled *Cosmic Rays* and *Cosmic Swirls,* I eliminated the landscape completely and just produced patterns made up of flowing lines and colors." As the images became more abstract, Tomchuk realized that she was responding to a whole new set of spatial and color features offered to her by satellite photos, moon photographs, rings around planets, the moons of Saturn and the like. They were very exciting to her because they represented heretofore unknown landscapes and objects in space.

During the last five years or so, Tomchuk's use of color has become ever more bold, exciting and innovative. Some of the colors arise spontaneously, at other times she puts a plate away for some weeks, months, or even a year. Both, formal as well as color problems, are often solved more easily after this 'rest period'. The artist relates one example of how she solved the 'color problem' for one print. "We had been to Boston

48

in late autumn and were driving along the shore passing many cranberry fields - they were all green. I thought it was rather odd for cranberry fields to be green when everyone knows that cranberries were really a rich red color. A few weeks before our Boston trip, I had been struggling with the colors of a new print. I had tried earth colors and considered some blues. After passing these green cranberry fields I suddenly knew what I was going to do with the obstreperous print. I was going to make it into a cranberry field which looked like a cranberry field. The image was that of a field and it only needed the inspiration for the color scheme to be used. Upon our return home, I mixed magentas, maroons and violets. In no time the print *Cranberry Field* was finished. It was just right, just the way I always wanted it to be!"

Tomchuk had at last found her very own creative style and imagery and celebrated this accomplishment by making a series of memorable prints such as *Fjord, High Tide,* the triptyches *Galaxy, Orbit* and many others.

In 1980, Tomchuk tackled yet another challenge: hand-made paper. She knew of no artist at the time who used handmade paper for printmaking. Most explorers of handmade paper created it and let it, the paper, be the art work. Others created color-pulp which they shaped into compositions and thus created their work of art. Tomchuk wanted to use handmade paper for her embossed prints because they would afford her deeper embossments. She took a weekend course in papermaking and received a lot of information in ten hours. "The problems with handmade paper are many. First of all, I had to determine what exactly it was I wanted to do with it and how I was going to control it and not have it control me. For about two to three years of experimentation it did control me."

One of the major problems is absorbency. Tomchuk's handmade paper is very thick and bulky; the ink is not totally absorbed into the inner structure of the paper. The paper made from 100% cotton, obtained from a mill in North Carolina, requires that the actual cotton fibers must be beaten to a pulp so as to use them in the papermaking process. "I wanted to keep the natural texture and lumpiness of the paper, because, after all, that is what gives it a lot of character. I did not want to make it into a super-refined sheet." Experiments with purchased handmade paper resulted in cracked paper when embossed. Tomchuk then ordered pulp from Twin Rocker in Indiana, and paid exorbitant freight charges because the pulp had to be shipped in water. She used the pulp to cast some reliefs which looked like exaggerated embossings. One day during this often discouraging period, she made some experimental sheets of paper, embossed them very, very deeply and, happily, they did not crack. Probably the greater thickness and less compression during the drying process kept the paper from cracking under the pressure of the press. She decided to make her own paper so as to achieve her stated goal of deeper embossment. Buying a pulp beater was as much a major and agonizing purchase as the Brand printing press. But once installed, Tomchuk is now able to make her own paper in her studio. She allows her paper to dry naturally, without the aid of a hydraulic press which squeezes out most of the water. This natural drying process retains the bumps and irregular surface textures. Some of them are reduced when put through the etching press for embossment but a lot of them remain. Once the cotton fibers dry in a rough texture, they tend to stay that way indefinitely.

Once the problems of papermaking had been solved, Tomchuk wanted to experiment further to find other uses, besides printmaking, for these sheets. She tried some dyed sheets of paper and made paintings against this background. It was fun for the former painter but really not very satisfying. Next came a few pieces of sculptured and collaged pieces in which she used a rope sandwiched between two pieces of pulp. She called this series Umbra I, II, and III. They were tedious and time-consuming to produce.

In 1983, Tomchuk at last started to make sheets of white handmade paper for use in embossed prints. One last hurdle had to be overcome. Applying color via inked plates through the press destroyed much of the fascinating textural qualities of the handmade paper. Tomchuk then began using an airbrush to apply color to the embossed prints. This is the method she uses to this day. It was in 1984 that Marjorie Tomchuk exhibited her embossed color prints on handmade paper for the first time. Admirers of her earlier work with embossed prints were exhilarated by this added step in the direction of achieving dramatic effects with the deeper embossment possible with the handmade paper. The beautiful naturally formed and exaggerated deckle edges look like torn paper but a closer inspection reveals that this is the normal look of handmade paper. A particularly impressive example is *Span* which also brings back associations with the earlier print *The Bridge*. The work remains abstract though carrying reality-oriented titles such as *Desert Road* and *Meteorite*. Some of the most accomplished and convincing work of the years since 1984 includes *Summer Breeze, Stellar Gate, Good Earth, Sonic Stream, Red Earth*, the diptyches *Seaway I & II*, and *Eclipse I & II*. Three of the most exciting prints dating from 1988 are *Red Planet, Solar Winds I*, and *Solar Winds II*.

Again two things felicitously flowed together. Tomchuk's embossed color prints on handmade paper in editions of 50, 75, and 100 were available for sale. Art directors, designers, buyers for corporations and individual collectors were enchanted by the work because it was novel, unique, beautifully produced in multiples and priced appropriately. It is rare that all of these factors come together in an artist's career: original creative work, a fascinating new technique, and buyer interest. What is the highest form of praise one can give at such a concatenation of factors is that it was achieved without compromising excellence, personal integrity, or artistic and aesthetic considerations.

No doubt Marjorie Tomchuk will extend her sights to new horizons as her ever curious eyes, mind, and restless hands continue to create. And we, her viewers, buyers and admirers will be the richer for it.

TECHNIQUES

WOODBLOCKS 1962-1964

The techniques described here are similar to the style of woodblock printing developed over the past 150 years by the artists of Japan.

The 'master' image is carved first, on a block or a board of bass plywood. Most often, this first woodcut becomes the structurally dominant color. Three or four good proofs are pulled and this first image is transferred to about three new blocks, for the creation of supporting color blocks. The proofs on paper are then painted freely by hand to determine location and intensity of colors and then each color is traced over unto the new woodblocks. Cutting of the new additional blocks proceeds with possible adjustments on all of them, keeping in mind the effectiveness of the dark, medium and light color areas. Proofing is made frequently to evaluate the 'look'. Each woodblock is always undercut to allow for later adjustments.

Watercolor paints are used for printing. The paper and the woodblocks must be maintained at the proper degree of dampness throughout of printing process. A wide variety of brushes are used to apply both water and ink to the surface of each woodcut.

Printing is done by hand with the use of a 'baren'. This is a round hard pad with a woven handle. It is used to transfer the image from the inked block to paper by rubbing the back of the paper which is placed face down. This baren is covered with a bamboo leaf in the traditional Japanese manner. Each color is printed unto a damp sheet until the entire edition is finished, background colors are first, the master block is printed last.

ETCHINGS 1965-1978

Beginning ideas or 'sources of inspiration' came from a store of photographs, sketches, and loose design ideas.

One image is selected and enlarged on tracing paper. Next, using ordinary carbon paper the drawing is transferred to a zinc or copper plate which earlier had been covered with an acid resistant coating. This will become the plate which carries the 'master' design, usually printed in black. The image is traced as a line drawing using a fine needle to cut through the acid resist, thus exposing the metal. A nitric acid bath etches into the line, or any area not protected by the resist. "Intaglio" prints carry the design by having ink embedded in the deep lines or depressed areas of the metal plate.

An alternative technique is photo engraving. Continuous tone film and line art are stripped together to form a montage. This is placed over photo sensitive resist, which covers a copper plate and is exposed to an arc lamp. The resist is hardened in the exposed non-printing areas, in preparation for etching with acid. The hardened area is not dissolved by the acid thus leaving the printing areas etched into the surface of the copper.

Working on an Etching Plate

Mixing Ink

Wiping the Plate with Tarlatan

Rolling Color Ink

After the first acid etch, the plate is cleaned and several proofs are pulled on the etching press. The artist generally sees areas which need change or adjustment. This is accomplished by traditional re-etching or using hand tools such as the scraper, burnisher, roulette wheel or engraving tools.With re-etching one or several of the following can be used: aquatint, hard or soft ground texture, sugar lift, cracking or open bite.

When inking a plate, heavy oil base etching ink is applied with a dauber to the entire surface of the etched plate. A stiffened cheesecloth, called tarlatan is rolled in a soft ball and used to wipe clean the surface, leaving ink only in the depressed areas.

Second and third state proofs serve as a guide to decide color areas. These are hand painted freely and later cut apart. The cutouts are pasted together or assembled as one collage. This method roughly indicates the color composition of the entire print. Tissues are then laid over each color area and positions are marked for making the final color plates.

The medium used for background color plates can vary, such as: another etched plate, linoleum, a collagraph or stiff smooth cardboard or a commercial lithographic plate. Colors are most often applied to these color plates with a roller. Friskets protect the large non-printing areas during inking. They are removed before printing and replaced for each subsequent inking. In some prints as many as six colors are used. Generally, the lightest color is printed first and the master plate is last. All plates are inked and printed in succession on damp paper.

The Artist,1968,Printing on an Etching Press

EMBOSSED PRINTS 1979-1983

The images which are found in this series of embossings have come from photographs of landscapes and seascapes and from random abstract sketches created by the artist.

This group of prints is more experimental in nature because the 'master' plate breaks away from use of the traditional metal plate, generally used for embossing. A deep plate is created slowly, not through acid-etching but by adding and subtracting design elements through the use of an industrial plastic. This medium can be equated to the consistency of clay in its 'leather-hard' state. Tools used to work out the image range from woodcut gouges, engraving tools, ceramic clay tools, and razor blades.

Several times during the creation of the master plate inkless proofs are pulled on the etching press, showing the embossing and the textural quality of the plate in progress. Later these same proofs are hand painted, indicating all the desired color areas.

Succeeding color plates are created by using the original proofs as a guide. Tracing paper marks the position of each color, and this shape is transferred to one of several mediums used for background plates, such as linoleum, zinc lithographic plates, stiff smooth cardboard or a collograph.

During printing these plates are surface rolled with etching or lithography inks. The lightest color is run through the press first, the deep embossing is always last. These plates are printed on dampened paper, in successive order so that a final, complete print is achieved. All the plates are re-inked for the next printing.

EMBOSSED PRINTS ON HANDMADE PAPER 1983-1989

There are three basic proceedures used in the creation of these prints: designing and producing a deep plate, making sheets of paper and applying color.

Techniques used in creating the embossed master plate remain the same as in the earlier version, dating back to 1979-83.

Paper making involves considerable equipment, such as a Hollander beater, papermaking molds, felt blankets, and vats, tubs or plastic trays.

Cotton linters, blotter like sheets of 100% cotton fibre are used to make pulp. Large quantities of water are used in the Hollander beater, where the naturally long fibres of cotton are cut, over a period of time and rotation. This freshly made pulp is then placed into a vat. A paper mold is used to lift a suitable amount out. Water drains from the screening of the mold and what remains is a pad of condensed pulp. The paper mold is then turned upside down and the firm pulp peels away from the screen. This

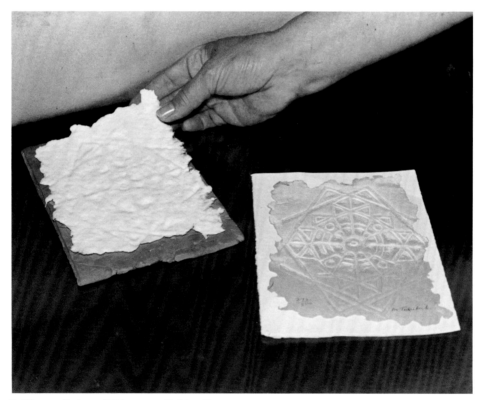

Pulling an Embossed Print on an Etching Press

step is referred to as 'couching'. The sheet is allowed to dry, natural air-drying creates a heavily textured surface.

For embossing, the master plate with its deeply recessed design is placed on an etching press. There is no color on the plate (inkless embossing). Prior to press work, the paper has been dampened with water. The heavy steel roller of the press exerts enough pressure on the paper and plate to create a deeply embossed image. Wet sheets are left to dry, the embossing remains permanent.

Water base paints, fabric dyes and pearlescent pigments are used to hand color each print, by means of an airbrush. Each color is applied to one sheet at a time, light colors are air brushed first, followed by graduating darks. On occasion a small area of color is applied by hand with a brush.

Making Pulp

Forming the Sheet

Couching

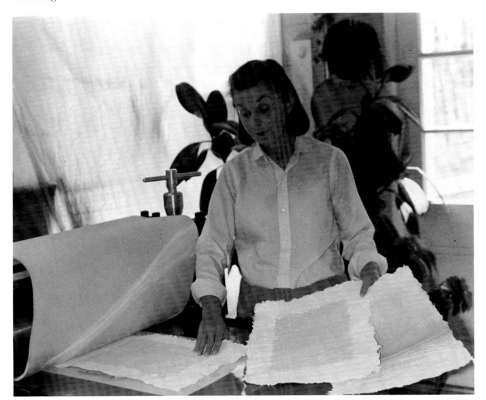

Embossing

Registering

Adding Color

CAST PAPER 1984-1989

Designing an image and choosing the type of sculptural mold to use is the first step in this process. The mold is made from plaster, styrofoam or plastic, depending on the 'look' desired.

After the mold has been designed and carved, a sufficient amount of pulp is made in the Hollander beater. This pulp is poured into the mold until an adequate thickness is built. Excess water is forced out with a sponge. This action also pushes the pulp fibres into the more delicate areas of the carving. A vacuum table or box can also be used to remove surplus water.

Cast paper takes several days to dry and when totally dry, it peels out of the mold with ease.

Art created as cast paper can be left in its pure white state. On some occasions these heavy relief pieces are painted with an airbrush in the same way as the limited edition prints.

CATALOGUE RAISONNÉ

All prints by M. Tomchuk were printed by the artist or assistant at her studio.

Each impression is titled, numbered and signed "M. Tomchuk" in pencil by the artist.

Sizes are in inches and (mm.) height before width.

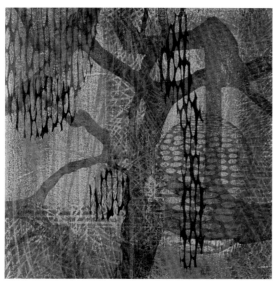

1 *Autumn* 1962
Woodcut
7 colors—brown, yellow-green, black, blue, mauve
17 x 17 (43.3 x 43.3 mm.)
Ed. 14
Hosho, woodblock paper

2 *Water Impression* 1962
Woodcut
8 colors—green, violet, blue, ochre
24 x 18 (61 x 45.5 mm.)
Ed. 6
Hosho, woodblock paper
Color plate page 5

3 *Greeting Card* 1962
Woodcut
3 colors—lt.blue, grey, silver
7 x 3¾ (18 x 9.5 mm.)
Open Ed.
Hosho, woodblock paper

4 *Dark Autumn* 1963
Woodcut
9 colors—grey-green, brown, black, yellow ochre, blue
22½ x 17½ (52 x 44.5 mm.)
Ed. 7
Hosho, woodblock paper

5 *Greeting Card* 1963
Woodcut
3 colors—tan, gold, green
7¼ x 3½ (18.5 x 9 mm.)
Open Ed.
Hosho, woodcut paper

6 *Angkor* 1964
Woodcut
5 colors—brown, beige, green, tan
22½ x 17½ (57 x 44.5 mm.)
Ed. 9
Hosho, woodcut paper

7 *Shiva* 1964
Shiva 2nd edition 1966
Woodcut
4 colors—gold, orange, yellow, green
23 x 17 (58.3 x 43 mm.)
Ed. 10, 16
Hosho, woodcut paper

8 *Kabuki Player* 1964
Woodcut
5 colors—blue, violet, black
24 x 18 (61 x 46 mm.)
Ed. 100
Hosho, woodcut paper

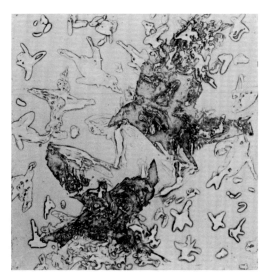

9   *Birds* 1964
Etching
2 colors—blue, black
12 x 12 (30.4 x 30.4 mm.)
Ed. 100
Dutch etching paper

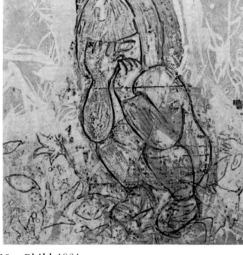

10   *Child* 1964
Etching
4 colors—yellow, green, brown, blue
12 x 12 (30.4 x 30.4 mm.)
Ed. 100
Italia paper

11   *Buddha* 1964
Etching
3 colors—black, green, grey
12 x 12 (30.4 x 30.4 mm.)
Ed. 100
Italia paper

12   *Monkeys* 1964
Etching
3 colors—yellow ochre, green, blue
12 x 12 (30.4 x 30.4 mm.)
Ed. 100
Dutch etching paper

13 _Indian Women_ 1964
Etching
3 colors—brown, green, ochre
12 x 12 (30.4 x 30.4 mm.)
Ed. 100
Italia paper

14 _Greeting Card_ 1964
Collograph
White paper, embossed
7 x 5 (18 x 13 mm.)
Open Ed.
Rives paper

15 _Taj Mahal_ 1965
Etching
5 colors—beige, blue, pink, grey, brown
12 x 12 (30.4 x 30.4 mm.)
Ed. 8
Dutch etching paper

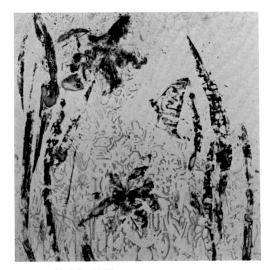

16 _Daffodils_ 1965
Etching
3 colors—yellow, green, blue
12 x 12 (30.4 x 30.4 mm.)
Ed. 100
Italia paper

17 *Arabian Horse* 1st State 1965
Arabian Horse 2nd State 1967
Etching
3 colors—yellow, ochre, orange, black
12 x 12 (30.4 x 30.4 mm.)
Ed. 8, 100
Partial edition commissioned by John Barton Associates Inc.
Collection: Davison Art Center, CT

18 *Angel* 1965
Etching
4 colors—yellow, green, red
12 x 12 (30.4 x 30.4 mm.)
Ed. 100
Italia paper

19 *Houses* 1962
Etching
3 colors—green, tan, brown
12 x 12 (30.4 x 30.4 mm.)
Ed. 100
Italia paper

20 *Peacocks* 1965
Etching
5 colors—turquoise, green, violet, black, ochre
12 x 12 (30.4 x 30.4 mm.)
Ed. 100
Italia paper

21 *Rose Window* 1965
Etching
5 colors—yellow, blue, red, brown, black
12 x 12 (30.4 x 30.4 mm.)
Ed. 100
Italia paper

22 *Greeting Card* 1965
Etching
2 colors—metallic gold, green
5 x 7 (14.5 x 18 mm.)
Open Ed.
Rives paper

23 *Reflections* 1966
Woodcut
9 colors—blue, yellow, grey, violet
24 x 18 (61 x 56 mm.)
Ed. 15
Hosho, woodblock paper

24 *Solo* 1966
Etching
2 colors—yellow ochre, blue
18 x 18 (46 x 46 mm.)
Ed. 100
Italia paper
Collection: Kantor, Shaw & Davidoff, N.Y., NY

25 *Spring Approaches Visibly* 1966
Woodcut
5 colors—grey, brown, yellow, green, turquoise
24 x 20 (61 x 51 mm.)
Ed. 100
Hosho woodcut paper

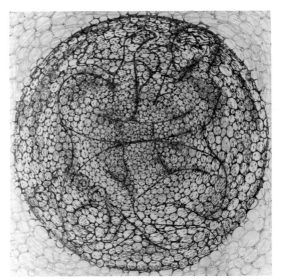

26 *Concentric Design* 1966
Etching
3 colors—brown, blue, tan
18 x 18 (46 x 46 mm.)
Ed. 100
Arches paper

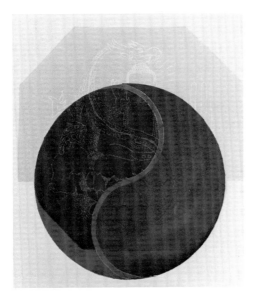

27 *Chinese Modern* 1966
Etching with embossing
4 colors—yellow, blue, magenta, green
19 x 17 (48 x 43 mm.)
Ed. 100
Italia paper

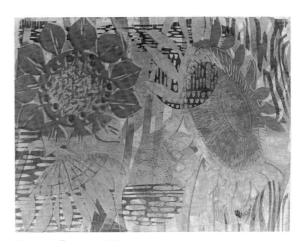

28 *Sunflowers* 1966
Woodcut
8 colors—silver, yellow, orange, blue
18 x 24 (46 x 61 mm.)
Ed. 15
Hosho, woodblock paper

29 *Greeting Card* 1966
Etching
1 color—red
7½ x 5½ (19 x 14 mm.)
Open Ed.
Metallic gold paper

30 *Spinning* 1967
Woodcut
5 colors—gold, red, green, black, brown
24 x 17½ (61 x 44.5 mm.)
Ed. 100
Hosho, woodblock paper

31 *Church* 1967
Etching
1 color—umber
7 x 3 (18 x 7.5 mm.)
Ed. 250
Italia paper

32 *Full Moon* 1967
Etching
3 colors—blue, yellow, pink
5½ x 3 (14 x 7.5 mm.)
Ed. 200
Italia paper

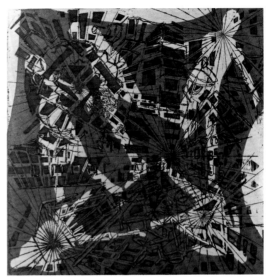

33 *Italy* 1967
Etching
2 colors—gold, black
9 x 5 (23 x 13 mm.)
Ed. 200
Italia paper

34 *Dark Canyons* 1967
Etching
3 colors—yellow, green, blue
18 x 18 (46 x 46 mm.)
Ed. 100
Italia paper

35 *Yellow Apple* 1967
also *Apple*, 2nd ed.
Etching
2 colors—yellow, black
2nd. ed: magenta, black
17½ x 17 (44.5 x 43 mm.)
Ed. 100
Italia paper

36 *Flight* 1967
Etching
2 colors—red, blue
18 x 18 (46 x 46 mm.)
Ed. 100
Italia paper

37 AVE. A, B, C, D, 1967
Etching
4 colors— tan, orange, green, black
17½ x 18 (44.5 x 46 mm.)
Ed. 100, 20 AP's
Italia paper
50 prints commissioned by New York Graphic Society
Collection: Hearst Publications, NY; Continental Group, CT
Winthrop, Stimson, Putnam & Roberts, N.Y., NY

38 The City 1967
Etching
4 colors—blue, yellow, green, black
18 x 15 (46 x 38 mm.)
Ed. 100
Italia paper

39 Landscape 1967
Etching
6 colors—yellow, blue, green, magenta, black
21 x 17½ (53.5 x 44.5 mm.)
Ed. 50
Italia paper

40 Eagle 1967
Etching
3 colors—red, blue, black
15 x 18 (38 x 49 mm.)
Ed. 100
Italia paper
Collection: Davison Art Center, CT

41 *Sunday in the Park* 1962
Etching
4 colors—yellow, green, vermillion, black
15 x 18 (38 x 46 mm.)
Ed. 100
Italia paper
50 prints commissioned by New York Graphic Society

42 *Two Women* 1967
Etching
3 colors—yellow ochre, tan, brown
15 x 18 (38 x 46 mm.)
Ed. 100
Italia paper
Collection: Charles Brand Co., NY

43 *Broadway* 1967
Etching
5 colors—yellow, orange, purple, green, black
20 x 16 (51 x 40.5 mm.)
Ed. 100
Italia paper
Collection: Davison Art Center, CT
M.L. Manor, MI

44 *Greeting Card* 1967
Woodcut, hand colored
6 colors—green, yellow, blue, red
4½ x 6 (12 x 15.5 mm.)
Open Ed.
Hosho, woodblock paper

45 *Mother and Child* 1968
Etching
4 colors—yellow, green, orange, black
18 x 15 (46 x 38 mm.)
Ed. 100, 20 AP's
Italia paper
Commissioned by Lublin Graphics Inc.

46 *Downtown* 1968
Etching
6 colors—yellow, grey, brown, black
20 x 16 (51 x 40.5 mm.)
Ed. 100
Italia paper
Collection: M. L. Manor, MI

47 *Greek Horseman* 1968
Etching
2 colors—red-brown, black
20 x 16 (51 x 40.5 mm.)
Ed. 100, 20 AP's
Italia paper
Commissioned by Lublin Gaphics Inc.
Collection: Champion Paper, Stamford, CT

48 *Prehistoric Bulls* 1968
Etching
4 colors—lt. blue, red ochre, yellow ochre, black
16 x 20 (40.5 x 51 mm.)
Ed. 100, 20 AP's
Italia paper
Commissioned by Lublin Graphics Inc.

49 *Theban Dancers* 1968
Etching
4 colors—yellow ochre, red ochre, tan, green
20 x 16 (51 x 40.5 mm.)
Ed. 100
Italia paper
Partial edition commissioned by John Barton Associates, Inc.
Collection: Kantor, Shaw & Davidoff, N.Y. NY

50 *Two Young People* 1968
Etching
5 colors—yellow, green, red ochre, sepia
16 x 20 (40.5 x 51 mm.)
Ed. 100
Italia paper

51 *The Chase* 1968
Etching
5 colors—blue, yellow ochre, red ochre, sepia, black
16 x 20 (40.5 x 51 mm.)
Ed. 100, 20 AP's
Italia paper
Commissioned by Lublin Graphics Inc.
Collection: Kantor, Shaw & Davidoff, N.Y., NY
Winthrup, Stimson, Putnam & Roberts, N.Y., NY

52 *Knight* 1968
Etching
3 colors—yellow ochre, black, red
20 x 16 (51 x 40.5 mm.)
Ed. 100, 10 AP's
Italia paper
Commissioned by John Barton Associates, Inc.

53 *Greeting Card* 1968
Woodcut
1 color—brown
also, some in metallic silver
4½ x 9¼ (11 x 23.5 mm.)
Open Ed.
Hosho, woodblock paper

54 *Assyrian Prince* 1969
Etching
2 colors—black, yellow ochre
16 x 16 (40.5 x 40.5 mm.)
Ed. 100, 10 AP's
Italia paper
Commissioned by Lublin Graphics, Inc

55 *Midtown* 1969
Etching
4 colors—green, orange, brown, black
5 x 3½ (13 x 9 mm.)
Ed. 100
Italia paper

56 *Sunflowers,* 2nd version 1969
Woodcut
9 colors—silver, yellow, green, orange, blue
18 x 24 (46 x 61 mm.)
Ed. 25
Hosho, woodcut paper

57 *Vikings* 1969
Etching
4 colors—yellow, green, crimson, black
20 x 16 (51 x 40.5 mm.)
Ed. 100, 20 AP's
Italia paper
Commissioned by John Barton Associates, Inc.
Collection: Winthrop, Stimson, Putnam & Roberts, N.Y., NY

58 *Young Girl* 1969
Etching
4 colors—yellow, tan, pink, black
18 x 15 (46 x 38 mm.)
Ed. 100, 20 AP's
Italia paper
Commissioned by Lublin Grahpics Inc.

59 *Mother and Daughter* 1969
Etching
3 colors—pink, red ochre, black
19 x 15 (46 x 38 mm.)
Ed. 100, 20 AP's
Italia paper
Commissioned by Lublin Graphics Inc.

60 *Epicenter* 1969
Etching
4 colors—blue, orange, brown, black
20 x 16 (51 x 40.5 mm.)
Ed. 100
Italia paper

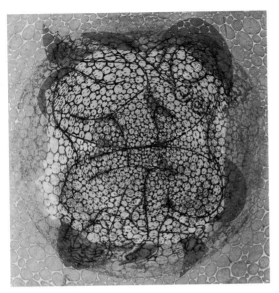

61 *Genesis* 1969
Etching
4 colors—blue, chartreuse, grey, black
18 x 18 (46 x 46 mm.)
Ed. 100
Italia paper
Collection: IBM Corporation

62 *Icarus* 1969
Embossed etching
2 colors—off-white, orange
18 x 18 (46 x 46 mm.)
Ed. 100, 20 AP's
Italia paper
Commissioned by Lublin Graphics Inc.
Collection: Wintrhup, Stimson, Putnam & Roberts, N.Y., NY

63 *King with Falcon* 1969
Embossed etching
6 colors—blue, red, ochre, sepia, black
18 x 18 (46 x 46 mm.)
Ed. 100, 20 AP's
Italia paper
Commissioned by Lublin Graphics Inc.
Collection: Kantor, Shaw & Davidoff, N.Y., NY

64 *Phoenix* 1969
Embossed etching
5 colors—yellow, orange, blue, brown
20 x 16 (51 x 40.5 mm.)
Ed. 100, 20 AP's
Italia paper
Commissioned by Lublin Graphics Inc.

65   *Dancers* 1969
Etching
5 colors—yellow ochre, red ochre, green, sepia
16 x 20
Ed. 100, 20 AP's
Italia paper

66   *Greeting Card* 1969
Etching with hand coloring
5 colors—metallic silver, red, blue, red, green
4 x 9 (9.5 x 22.5 mm.)
Open Ed.
Hosho, woodblock paper

67   *Abracadabra* 1970
Embossed etching
5 colors—green, yellow, red, black
20 x 16 (51 x 40.5 mm.)
No Ed. 10 AP's
Italia paper

68   *Noah's Ark* 1970
Embossed etching
3 colors—turquoise, chartruese, black
18 x 18 (46 x 46 mm.)
Ed. 50, 10 AP's
Italia paper
Commissioned by Ferdinand Roten Galleries, Inc., Baltimore, MD
Collection: New Canaan Bank & Trust Co., CT;
Kantor, Shaw & Davidoff, N.Y., NY

69 *Theseus in the Labyrinth* 1970
Embossed etching
3 colors—yellow, brown, black
18 x 18 (46 x 46 mm.)
Ed. 100, 20 AP's
German etching paper
Commissioned by Lublin Graphics Inc.
Collection: Kantor, Shaw & Davidoff, N.Y., NY;
Winthrup, Stimson, Putnam & Roberts, N.Y., NY

70 *Astronomer* 1970
Embossed etching
4 colors—blue, off-white, yellow ochre, sepia
24 x 18 (61 x 46 mm.)
Ed. 100, 20 AP's
German etching paper
Commissioned by Lublin Graphics Inc.
Collection: Wintrhup, Stimson, Putnam & Roberts, N.Y., NY

71 *Sachem* 1970
Etching
4 colors—yellow, brown, blue, black
18 x 18 (46 x 46 mm.)
Ed. 100, 20 AP's
Italia paper
Commissioned by Lublin Graphics Inc.
Collection: Museum of Native Amerrican Cultures, Spokane, WA;
New Canaan Bank & Trust Co., New Canaan, CT

72 *Venus* 1970
Etching
4 colors—off-white, lt. green, ochre, black
18 x 15 (46 x 38 mm.)
Ed. 100, 20 AP's
Italia paper
Commissioned by Lublin Graphics Inc.

89 *The Divine Sarah* 1971
Etching
6 colors—yellow, blue, tan, red, brown, black
20 x 16 (51 x 40.5 mm.)
Ed. 100, 20 AP's
Italia paper
Commissioned by Lublin Graphics Inc.
Collection: Newark Museum, Newark, NJ

90 *Greeting Card* 1971
Etching
1 color—lt. tan
5 x 4 (12.5 x 10 mm.)
Open Ed.
German Etching paper

91 *Silvermine Guild Poster* 1972
Embossed etching
2 colors—yellow, turquoise
22 x 18 (56 x 46 mm.)
Ed. 175
Arches paper
Commissioned by the Silvermine Guild of Artists, 50th Anniversary

92 *Peanut Cart* 1st state 1972
***Peanut Cart on Larimer Square* 2nd state**
Etching
2 colors—cream, black
5 colors—cream, tan, yellow, red, black
16 x 20 (40.5 x 51 mm.)
Ed. 100, 20 AP's
Italia paper
Both commissioned by Lublin Graphics Inc.
2nd State:
Selected and cataloged by the Original Print Collectors Group, NY
Collection: The Denver Art Museum, CO; DeCordova Museum, MA;
University Club of Chicago, IL
Award: Purchase Prize, DeCordova Museum, Lincoln, MA

93   *Greeting Card* 1972
Etching
3 colors—lt. blue, yellow, tan
4 x 5 (10 x 12.5 mm.)
Open Ed.
German Etching paper

94   *From Another Era* 1973
Memorial to an Era 2nd state
Etching
5 colors—yellow, red, ochre, black
2 colors—cream, black
20 x 16 (51 x 40.5 mm.)
Ed. 100, 20 AP's
Italia paper
Commissioned by Lublin Graphics Inc.
Collection: 2nd state: Library of Congress, Wash., DC;
The Butler Institute of American Art, Youngstown, OH
Award: Stamford Art Association, 1st Prize
Color plate page 33

95   *Old Number Three* 1973
Etching
4 colors—red, blue, yellow, black
20 x 16 (51 x 40.5 mm.)
Ed. 100, 20 AP's
Italia paper
Commissioned by Lublin Graphics Inc.

96   *Paul Revere* 1973
Etching
5 colors—cream, ochre, turquoise, brown, black
20 x 16 (51 x 40.5 mm.)
Ed. 100, 20 AP's
Arches paper
Partial edition commissioned by Lublin Graphics Inc.
Collection: New Canaan Bank & Trust Co., CT

97 *Greeting Card* 1973
Etching
2 colors—turquoise, yellow
4 x 5 (10 x 12.5 mm.)
Open Ed.
Arches paper

98 *Vieux Carré* 1974
Etching
6 colors—cream, blue, red, yellow, black
20 x 16 (51 x 40.5 mm.)
Ed. 100, 20 AP's
Italia paper
Partial edition commissioned by Lublin Graphics Inc.
Color plate page 37

99 *Apothecary* 1974
Etching
7 colors—cream, lt. blue, borwn, yellow, red, sepia
20 x 16 (51 x 40.5 mm.)
Ed. 100, 20 AP's
Arches paper, buff
Partial edition commissioned by Lublin Graphics Inc.

100 *Mystic Seaport* 1974
Etching
9 colors—yellow, orange, red, green, blue, turquoise, black
16 x 20 (40.5 x 51 mm.)
Ed. 100, 20 AP's
Italia paper
Partial edition commissioned by Lublin Graphics Inc.
Collection: University Club of Chicago, IL'
New Canaan Bank & Trust Co., CT

101 *Sunshine and Lace* 1974
Etching
5 colors—cream, yellow, orange, green, sepia
24 x 18 (61 x 46 mm.)
Ed. 100, 20 AP's
Italia paper
Partial edition commissioned by Lublin Graphics Inc.

102 *Greeting Card* 1974
Etching
2 colors—crimson, yellow
4 x 5 (10 x 12.5 mm.)
Open Ed.
Arches paper

103 *Ghirardelli Square* 1975
Etching over lithography
4 colors—yellow, orange, blue, black
24 x 18 (61 x 46 mm.)
Ed. 100, 20 AP's
Arches paper
Partial edition commissioned by Lublin Graphics Inc.

104 *State Fair* 1975
Etching over lithography
6 colors—green, blue, orange, red, black
24 x 18 (61 x 46 mm.)
Ed. 100, 20 AP's
Arches paper
Partial edition commissioned by Lublin Graphics Inc.
Collection: New Canaan Bank & Trust Co., CT

105 *Grand Victorian* 1975
Relief etching
3 colors—yellow, lt. turquoise, maroon
24 x 18 (61 x 46 mm.)
Ed. 100, 20 AP's
Arches paper
Partial edition commissioned by Lublin Graphics Inc.
Color plate page 37

106 *Greeting Card* 1975
Etching
2 colors—lt. tan, tan
5 x 4 (12.5 x 10 mm.)
Open Ed.
German Etching paper

107 *View from the Ferry* 1976
Etching over lithography
3 colors—lt. yellow, med, yellow, black
24 x 18 (61 x 46 mm.)
Ed. 120, 20 AP's
Arches paper
Collection: Museum of the City of New York, NY; Winthrup, Stimson,
    Putnam & Roberts, N.Y., NY;
Western Electric, N.Y., NY
Color plate page 36

108 *Snow Crystal* 1976
Etching
4 colors—turquoise, yellow, crimson, black
19½ x 17½ (49.5 x 44.5 mm.)
Ed. 120, 20 AP's
Italia paper

109   *The Bridge* 1976
Etching
4 colors—turquoise, yellow, black
19½ x 17½ (49.5 x 44.5 mm.)
Ed. 120, 20 AP's
Italia paper
Color plate page 33

110   *Greeting Card* 1976
Etching
2 colors—blue, yellow
5 x 4 (12.5 x 10 mm.)
Open Ed.
Italia paper

111   *Chrysanthemums* 1977
Embossed etching
5 colors—yellow, lt. blue, green, brown
20 x 16 (51 x 40.5 mm.)
Ed. 150, 20 AP's
Italia paper
Commissioned by Original Print Collectors Group, NY

112   *Reflection* 1977
Etching
3 colors—cream, red ochre, sepia
20 x 16 (51 x 40.5 mm.)
Ed. 120, 20 AP's
Italia paper

113 *Spring Bouquet* 1977
Embossed etching
5 colors—orange, pink, yellow, green, tan
20 x 16 (51 x 40.5 mm.)
Ed. 150, 30 AP's
Italia paper

114 *Trail's End* 1977
Etching
4 colors—lt. blue, yellow, brown, black
19½ x 17½ (49.5 x 44.5 mm.)
Ed. 150, 30 AP's
Arches paper
Collection: Nelson Gallery of Art, Kansas City, MO

115 *On the Plains* 1977
Relief etching
5 colors—lt. blue, ochre, red, brown, black
24 x 18 (61 x 46 mm.)
Ed. 150, 25 AP's
Arches paper

116 *Ceremonial* 1977
Relief etching
4 colors—red ochre yellow, tan, sepia
24 x 18 (61 x 46 mm.)
No Ed., 10 AP's
Arches paper

117 *Greeting Card* 1977
Etching
1 color—red, embossed
8 x 2½ (20 x 6.5 mm.)
Open Ed.
Arches paper

118 *Shield* 1978
Relief etching
5 colors—brown, ochre, blue, red, black
24 x 18 (61 x 46 mm.)
Ed. 150, 25 AP's
Arches paper

119 *Country Store* 1978
Etching
4 colors—blue, red, yellow, black
19½ x 17½ (49.5 x 44.5 mm.)
Ed. 150, 30 AP's
Arches paper

120 *Aces* 1978
Etching
5 colors—ochre, yellow, lt. blue, red, black
24 x 18 (61 x 46 mm.)
Ed. 150, 25 AP's
Arches paper
Collection: Winthrup, Stimson, Putnam & Roberts, N.Y., NY

121 *Indian Girl* 1978
Relief etching
3 colors—yellow, tan, sepia
24 x 18 (61 x 46 mm.)
Ed. 150, 25 AP's
Arches paper

122 *Art '78 Poster* 1978
Linocut
2 colors—yellow, brown
28 x 20 (71 x 51 mm.)
Open Ed.
Arches paper
Commissioned by Olejniczak Gallery

123 *Greeting Card* 1978
Etching
Embossing on silver foil
5 x 4 (12.5 x 10 mm.)
Open Ed.
Arches paper

124 *Bison* 1979
Mixed media, embossed
5 colors—lt. yellow, green, ochre, sepia
24 x 20 (61 x 51 mm.)
Ed. 150, 30 AP's
Arches paper

125 *Unicorn* 1979
Mixed media, embossed
5 colors—cream, yellow, orange, red ochre, sepia
24 x 20 (61 x 51 mm.)
Ed. 150, 30 AP's
Arches paper
Collection: Professional Liability Underwriting Managers
(PLUM) MN; Dr. Elisabeth Caraffa, Hawthorn Children's
Psychiatric Hospital, St. Louis, MO

126 *Athena* 1979
Mixed media, embossed
4 colors—yellow, yellow ochre, orange, sepia
24 x 20 (61 x 51 mm.)
Ed. 150, 30 AP's
Arches paper

127 *Ocean* 1979
Mixed media, embossed
6 colors—blue, turquoise, coral, pink, sepia
24 x 20 (61 x 51 mm.)
Ed. 150, 30 AP's
Arches paper
Collection: Anheuser-Busch Inc., St. Louis, MO;
Shore Memorial Hospital, Somers Point, NJ;
1st Exchange Bank, St. Louis, MO; Emerson Electric, MO;
Veda Inc., Arlington, VA; Dr. Lydia David, NJ

128 *Dunes* 1979
Mixed media, embossed
5 colors—beige, coral, blue, sepia
24 x 20 (61 x 51 mm.)
Ed. 150, 30 AP's
Arches paper
Collection: Emerson Electric, St. Louis, MO;
First Exchange Bank, St. Louis, MO;
True Temper Sports, TN

129 *Dawn* 1979
Mixed media, embossed
3 colors—lt. green, orange, sepia
24 x 20 (61 x 51 mm.)
Ed. 150, 30 AP's
Arches paper

130 *Sky Symphony* 1979
Mixed media, embossed
5 colors—cream, lt. turquoise, blue, yellow, orange
24 x 20 (61 x 51 mm.)
Ed. 150, 30 AP's
Arches paper
Collection: 1st Exchange Bank, St. Louis, MO

131 *Soaring* 1979
Mixed media, embossed
2 colors—lt. blue, cream
E. 150, 30 AP's
Arches paper

132 *Blue Panther* 1979
Mixed media, embossed
6 colors—red ochre, sepia, lt. blue, blue, cream, mauve
24 x 20 (61 x 51 mm.)
Ed. 150, 30 AP's
Arches paper

133 *Great Oak* 1979
Mixed media, embossed
3 colors—turquoise, yellow, green
24 x 20 (61 x 51 mm.)
Ed. 150, 30 AP's
Arches paper

134 *Eventide* 1979
Mixed media, embossed
4 colors—coral, beige, grey, blue
24 x 20 (61 x 51 mm.)
Ed. 150, 30 AP's
German etching paper
Collection: General American Life Insurance Co.,
St. Louis, MO; Veda Inc. Arlington, VA

135 *Timberline* 1979
Mixed media, embossed
5 colors—yellow, grey, green
24 x 20 (61 x 51 mm.)
Ed. 150 30 AP's
Arches paper
Collection: Anhueser-Busch Inc., MO;
1st Exchange Bank, St. Louis, MO;
General American Life Insurance Co., Nat. Hdqtrs., St. Louis, MO;
Wilton High School, Wilton, CT

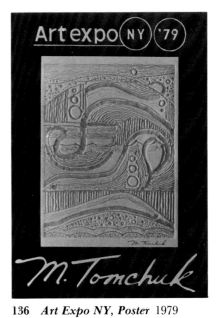

136 *Art Expo NY, Poster* 1979
Mixed media, embossed
2 colors—turquoise, grey
21½ x 15½ (54.5 x 39 mm.)
Open Ed.
Promatco paper
Collection: New England Center for Contemporary Art,
Brooklyn, CT

137   *World Art Expo, Boston, Poster* 1979
Mixed media, embossed
1 color—tan
21½ x 15½ (54.5 x 39 mm.)
Open Ed.
Promatco paper
Collection: Richmond Art Gallery, Richmond, B.C., Canada;
New England Center for Contemporary Art, Brooklyn, CT

138   *Wash Art Poster* 1979
Mixed media, embossed
2 colors—rust, tan
21½ x 16½ (54.5 x 39 mm.)
Open Ed.
Promatco paper

139   *Greeting Card* 1979
Etching
3 colors—yellow, orange, green
5 x 4 (12.5 x 10 mm.)
Open Ed.
Italia paper

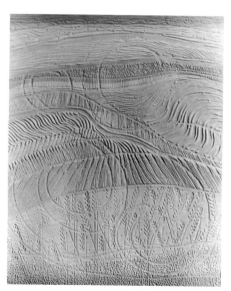

140   *Wheatfields* 1979
Mixed media, embossed
5 colors—yellow, ochre, turquoise, brown
24 x 20 (61 x 51 mm.)
Ed. 150, 30 AP's
German Etching paper
Collection: General American Life Insurance Co., MO
Color plate page 13

141 *Summer Solstice* 1979
Mixed media, embossed
7 colors—yellow, blue, mauve, grey
24 x 20 (61 x 51 mm.)
Ed. 150, 30 AP's
German Etching paper
Collection: General American Life Insurance Co., MO;
Anheuser-Busch Inc., MO; Dr. Lydia David, NJ;
Simon Barcham Green, Hayle Mill, Kent, England

142 *Canyon* 1979
Mixed media, embossed
6 colors—brown, blue, yellow, orange
24 x 20 (61 x 51 mm.)
Ed. 150, 30 AP's
German Etching paper
Collection: Emerson Electric, St. Louis, MO;
First Exchange Bank, St. Louis, MO;
Veda Inc., Arlington, VA

143 *Cascade* 1979
Mixed media, embossed
2 colors—lt. green, grey
24 x 20 (61 x 51 mm.)
Ed. 150, 30 AP's
Arches paper
Collection: The Residence Inn, Marriott Corp.,
Binghamton, NY

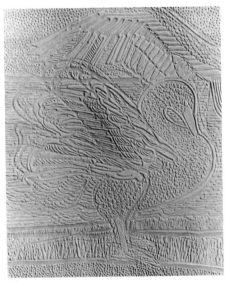

144 *Swan* 1980
Mixed media, embossed
4 colors—off white, grey, tan
24 x 20 (61 x 51 mm.)
Ed. 150, 30 AP's
German Etching paper

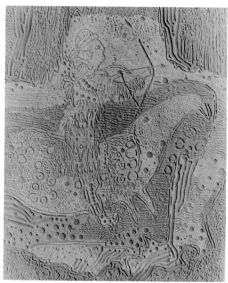

145 *Horseman* 1980
Mixed media, embossed
5 colors—off-white, yellow, brown, grey
24 x 20 (61 x 51 mm.)
Ed. 150, 30 AP's
German Etching paper

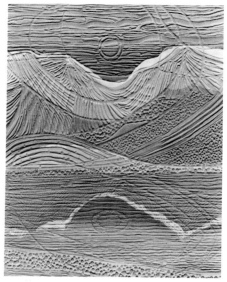

146 *Sandhills* 1980
Mixed media, embossed
5 colors—tan, orange, yellow, blue
24 x 20 (61 x 51 mm.)
Ed. 150, 30 AP's
German Etching paper
Collection: Veda Inc., Arlington, VA; True Temper
Sports, TN

147 *October Landscape* 1980
Mixed media, embossed
6 colors—red, yellow, tan
24 x 20 (61 x 51 mm.)
Ed. 150, 30 AP's
German Etching paper
Collection: Ontario Government, Service Department Branch,
Toronto, Canada; General American Life Insurance Co., MO;
True Temper Sports, TN

148 *Greeting Card* 1980
Linocut
2 colors—lt. green, grey
5 x 4 (12.5 x 10 mm.)
Open Ed.
Italia paper

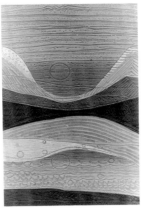

149 *Sierra* (quartet) 1980

Mixed media, embossed
6 colors—tan, brown, yellow, orange, lt. blue
31 x 88 (79 x 224 mm.)
Ed. 150, 30 AP's
German Etching paper
Collection: Ontario Government, Ministry of Energy, Toronto;
Robin Hood Multi Foods, Hdqtrs, Toronto, Canada;
The Hammond Clinic, IN; True Temper Sports, TN;
Camelback Inn, OK
Color plate page 12

150 *Fjord* 1980

Mixed media, embossed
6 colors—green, brown, tan turquoise
24 x 20 (61 x 51 mm.)
Ed. 150, 30 AP's
German Etching paper
Collection: New Canaan Library, CT;
Ontario Government, Service Development Branch,
Toronto Canada

151 *Coral Sky* 1980

Mixed media, embossed
5 colors—orange, tan, rust, green, yellow
24 x 20 (61 x 51 mm.)
Ed. 150, 30 AP's
German Etching paper
Collection: First Exchange Bank, St. Louis, MO;
Emerson Electric, St. Louis, MO; Veda Inc., Arlington, VA;
The Hammond Clinic, IN; Dr. Lydia David, NJ

152　High Tide 1980
Mixed media, embossed
6 colors—grey, turquoise, blue, yellow, orange
24 x 20 (61 x 51 mm.)
Ed. 150, 30 AP's
German Etching paper

153　Aleutian Island 1980
Mixed media, embossed
6 colors—mauve, turquoise, blue, yellow
24 x 20 (61 x 51 mm.)
Ed. 150, 30 AP's
German Etching paper

 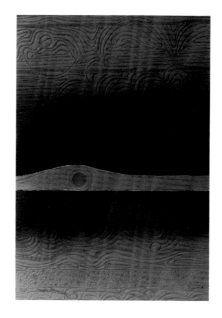

154　Pacific Storm I & II 1980
Mixed media, embossed
6 colors—blue, turquoise, grey, yellow, orange
31 x 44 (79 x 112 mm.)
Ed. 150, 30 AP's
German Etching paper
Collection: Veda Inc., Arlington, VA

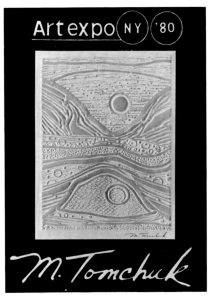

155   *Art Expo NY Poster* 1980
Mixed media, embossed
2 colors—brown, tan
21½ x 15½ (54.5 x 39 mm.)
Open Ed.
Promatco paper

156   *Prints 80 Poster* 1980
Mixed media, embossed
2 colors—yellow ochre, tan
21½ x 15½ (54.5 x 39 mm.)
Open Ed.
Promatco paper

157   *Art Expo West, Poster* 1980
Mixed media, embossed
3 colors—pale green, yellow, tan
21½ x 15½ (54.5 x 39 mm.)
Open Ed.
Promatco paper

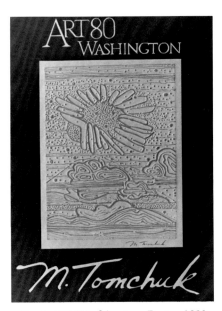

158   *Art 80 Washington, Poster* 1980
Mixed media, embossed
2 colors—red-violet, tan
21½ x 15½ (54.5 x 39 mm.)
Open Ed.
Promatco paper

159 *North Ridge I, II, III* 1980
Mixed media, embossed
7 colors—turquoise, blue, mauve, yellow
24 x 20 (61 x 51 mm.) each
Ed. 150, 30 AP's
German Etching paper
Collection: Ontario Gov't Ministry of Energy, Toronto, Canada;
The Hammond Clinic, IN

160 *Dartmouth '54* 1981
Etching
4 colors—green, lt. green, tan, black
19½ x 17½ (49.5 x 44.5 mm.)
Ed. 54
Arches paper
Commissioned by Dartmouth alumni as the "Class of '54 Award"
Collection: Rockefeller Social Science Building, Dartmouth
College, NH

161 *Greeting Card* 1981
Etching
6 colors—violet, blue, green, yellow, orange
5 x 4 (12.5 x 10 mm.)
Open Ed.
Italia paper

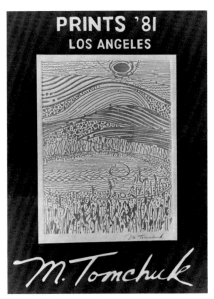

162   *Prints 81 Poster* 1981
Mixed media, embossed
5 colors—green, blue, yellow, tan
21½ x 15½ (54.5 x 39 mm.)
Open Ed.
Promatco paper

163   *Art Expo NY Poster* 1981
Mixed media, embossed
4 colors—tan, rose, magenta, blue
21½ x 15½ (54.5 x 39 mm.)
Open Ed.
Promatco paper

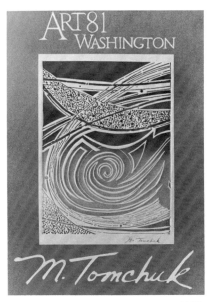

164   *Art 81 Washington, Poster* 1981
Mixed media, embossed
4 colors—blue, mauve, dk. yellow
21½ x 15½ (54.5 x 39 mm.)
Open Ed.
Promatco paper
Collection: Library of Congress, Poster Collection, Wash., DC

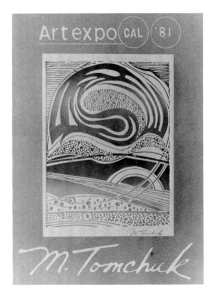

165   *Art Expo Cal Poster* 1981
Mixed media, embossed
5 colors—coral, grey, blue, tan
21½ x 15½ (54.5 x 39 mm.)
Open Ed.
Promatco paper

166 *Breakers I & II* 1981
Cast paper
Color: white
23 x 18½ (58 x 47 mm.)
Ed. 75
Artist-made paper

167 *Waves I & II* 1981
Cast paper
Color: white
17½ x 14½ (45 x 37 mm.)
Ed. 75
Artist-made paper

168   *Thundercloud* 1982
Mixed media, embossed
6 colors—blue, grey-green, yellow, orange
24 x 20 (61 x 51 mm.)
Ed. 150 30 AP's
German Etching paper

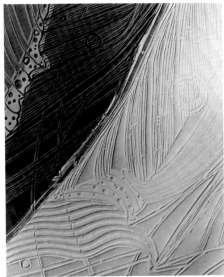

169   *Boundary* 1982
Mixed media, embossed
7 colors—tan, brown, turquoise, red ochre
24 x 20 (61 x 54 mm.)
Ed. 150 30 AP's
German Etching paper
Collection: Veda Inc., Arlington, VA

170   *Lava Field* 1982
Mixed media, embossed
6 colors—red-brown, orange, yellow, cream
24 x 20 (61 x 51 mm.)
Ed. 150, 30 AP's
German Etching paper
Collection: American Standard Corp., NJ

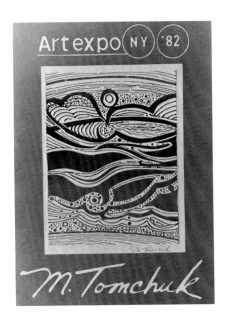

171   *Art Expo NY Poster* 1982
Mixed media, embossed
5 colors—green, grey, yellow, red, orange
21½ x 15½ (54.5 x 39 mm.)
Open Ed.
Promatco paper

172 *Strata I & II* 1982
Mixed media, embossed
6 colors—brown, tan, ochre, pink, off-white, lt. blue
24 x 40 (61 x 102 mm.)
Ed. 150, 30 AP's
German Etching paper
Collection: True Temper Sports, TN

173 *Greeting Card* 1982
Etching
3 colors—magenta, blue, yellow
5 x 4 (12.5 x 10 mm.)
Open Ed.
Italia paper

174 *Sunset* 1982
Mixed media, embossed
6 colors—blue, mauve, maroon, red, yellow, orange
24 x 20 (61 x 51 mm.)
Ed. 150, 30 AP's
German Etching paper
Collection: First Exchange Bank, St. Louis, MO; Orthopedic Surgeons
& Sports Medicine, Camp Hill, PA

175 *Star Cluster* 1982
Mixed media, embossed
5 colors—tan, grey, maroon, beige, off-white
24 x 20 (61 x 51 mm.)
Ed. 150, 30 AP's
German Etching paper
Collection: Veteran's Adminstration, IL;
Veda Inc., Arlington, VA

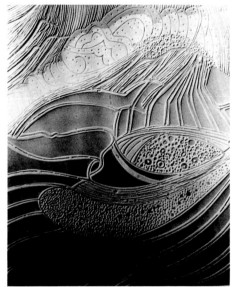

176 *Whitecap* 1982
Mixed media, embossed
5 colors—dk. blue, turquoise, grey, yellow, lt. blue
24 x 20 (61 x 51 mm.)
Ed. 150, 30 AP's
German Etching paper
Collection: Dr. Elisabeth Caraffa, Hawthorn Children's
Psychiatric Hospital, St. Louis, MO

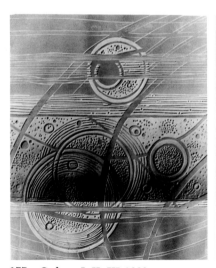

177 *Galaxy I, II, III* 1982
Mixed media, embossed
5 colors—grey, purple, red, magenta, yellow
24 x 60 (61 x 153 mm.)
Ed. 150
German Etching paper
Collection: Allstate, Northbrook, IL; Veda Inc., Arlington, VA

217   *Red Earth* 1984
Mixed media, embossed
4 colors—red ochre, red, black, cream
25 x 36
Ed. 100, 10 AP's
Artist-made paper
Collection: Vanguard Atlantic Ltd., NY

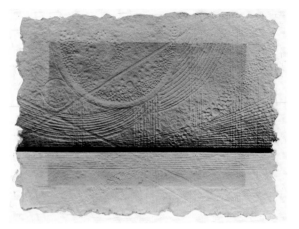

218   *Stellar Gate* 1985
Mixed media, embossed
4 colors—tan, grey, maroon, cream
25 x 36
Ed. 100, 10 AP's
Artist-made paper
Collection: National Bank of Washington, DC; E.I. DuPont, NJ;
Chancellor Capital Corp., TX; Blue Cross/Blue Shield, VA;
Arundel Communications Inc., VA; Burnup & Sims, FL;
Facciani & Co., Independence, OH; The Residence,
Marriott Corp., Richmond, VA
Color plate page 48

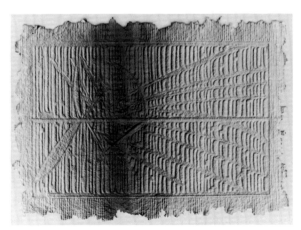

219   *Radials* 1985
Mixed media, embossed
3 colors—brown, tan, black
25 x 36 (63.5 x 91 mm.)
Ed. 100, 10 AP's
Artist-made paper
Collection: Veteran's Administration, Chicago, IL

220   *Early Dawn* 1985
Mixed media, embossed
4 colors—coral, lt. yellow, blue, mauve
25 x 36 (63.5 x 91 mm.)
Ed. 100, 10 AP's
Artist-made paper
Collection: Faccianni & Co., Independence, OH

221   *Ebbtide* 1985
Mixed media, embossed
6 colors—shades of green, grey, mauve, peach, black
36 x 25 (91 x 63.5 mm.)
Ed. 100, 10 AP's
Artist-made paper
Collection: Corporate Art Services, Kansas City, MO
Color plate page 1

222   *Moonscape* 1985
Mixed media, embossed
5 colors—blue, grey, black, tan, off-white
36 x 25 (91 x 63.5 mm.)
Ed. 100, 10 AP's
Artist-made paper
Collection: Hewlett – Packard Co., VA;
Visconsi Management Co., OH; Vanguard Atlantic Ltd., NY

223   *Contrails I & II* 1985
Mixed media, embossed
5 colors—tan, lt. yellow, grey, blue, rust
25 x 72 (63.5 x 182 mm.)
Ed. 100, 10 AP's
Artist-made paper
Collection: General Electric, CT; Bell Labs, Chicago, IL;
United Monetary Group, TX; Federal Express, TN;
New England Bell, CT; Bell Atlantic, Silver Spring, MD;
Xerox Corp., NY; Southwestern Bell; Playtex International, CT;
Arundel Communications Inc., VA; McCollister Moving & Storage
Hdqtrs., NJ; Sabin, Bermant & Gould, NY; T-Bar Corp., CT;
Technical Documentation Services, MN

224 *Eclipse I & II* 1985
Mixed media, embossed
5 colors—blue, grey, black, tan, off-white
36 x 50 (91 x 127 mm.)
Ed. 100, 10 AP's
Artist-made paper
Collections: American Standard Corp., NJ; General Accident
Insurance, Il; Bell & Howell, IL; Tanable USA Inc., NJ;
Hewlett Packard Co., VA; Vanguard Atlantic Ltd., NY;
Riverside Publishing, IL; Continental Webb, IL; Bunker Ramo, CT;
First Family Mortgage, IL; Lagastee Insurance Agency, IL;
The Residence Inn, Marriott Corp., NY
Color plate pages 8, 9

225 *Greeting Card* 1985
Linocut
1 color—mauve
6 x 4 (15 x 10 mm.)
Ed. 500
Artist-made paper

226 *Coral Reef* 1986
Mixed media, embossed
4 colors—pink, mauve, lt. green, blue-violet
36 x 25 (91 x 63.5 mm.)
Ed. 100, 10 AP's
Artist-made paper
Collection: American Communications, IL;
Connecticut Bank & Trust Co., CT;
Risk Management, Grand Rapids, MI

227 *Seaway I & II* 1986
Mixed media, embossed
6 colors—peach, grey, turquoise, grey-green, violet
36 x 50 (91 x 127 mm.)
Ed. 100, 10 AP's
Artist-made paper
Collection: O'Sullivan, Beauchamp, Kelly & Whipple, Port Huron, MI
Color plate page 40

228 *Summit I & II* 1986
Mixed media, embossed
4 colors—grey, rose, blue, tan
36 x 50 (91 x 127 mm.)
Ed. 100, 10 AP's
Artist-made paper
Collection: Counselor Realty, MN

229 *Shell* 1986
Mixed media, embossed
3 colors—peach, cream, pearlescent russet
36 x 25 (91 x 63.5 mm.)
Ed. 100, 10 AP's
Artist-made paper
Commissioned by Xerox Corp. Stamford, CT, as
a single piece, cast paper original

230 *Dusk* 1986
Mixed media, embossed
4 colors—pink, mauve, green, blue-violet
14 x 10 (35.5 x 25.5 mm.)
Ed. 50,10 AP's
Artist-made paper
Commissioned by Isetan Gallery, Tokyo, Japan

231 *Eterna I & II* 1986
Mixed media, embossed
4 colors—tan, grey, peach, silver
36 x 50 (91 x 127 mm.)
Ed. 100, 10 AP's
Artist-made paper

232　Greeting Card 1986
Etching
3 colors—pink, lt. blue, pearlescent white
6 x 4 (14 x 10 mm.)
Ed. 400
Artist-made paper

233　Spectrum 1986
Mixed media, embossed
8 colors—shades of violet, magenta, mauve
36 x 25 (71 x 63.5 mm.)
Ed. 100, 10 AP's
Artist-made paper

234　Galley 1987
Mixed media, embossed
4 colors—peach, yellow, blue, rust
14 x 19 (35.5 x 48 mm.)
Ed. 75, 10 AP's
Artist-made paper

235　Summer Breeze 1987
Mixed media, embossed
5 colors—pink, violet, green, grey, peach
14 x 19 (35.5 x 48 mm.)
Ed. 75, 10 AP's
Artist-made paper
Collection: The Print Consortium, St. Joseph, MO
Color plate page 16

236 *Butte, Red Butte* 1987
Mixed media, embossed
4 colors—blue, pink, tan, peach
14 x 19 each (35.5 x 48 mm.)
Ed. 75, 10 AP's
Artist-made paper

237 *Harmony* 1987
Mixed media, embossed
4 colors—mauve, pink, peach, yellow
14 x 19 (35.5 x 48 mm.)
Ed. 75, 10 AP's
Artist-made paper

238 *Greeting Card* 1987
Etching
1 color—pearlescent silver
6 x 4 (14 x 10 mm.)
Ed. 400
Artist-made paper

239 *Fronds* 1987
Mixed media, embossed
5 colors—green, turquoise, tan, pink, rose
14 x 19 (35.5 x 48 mm.)
Ed. 75, 10 AP's
Artist-made paper

240 *Marquee* 1988
Mixed media, embossed
4 colors—grey, black, tan, red
25 x 36 (63.5 x 91 mm.)
Ed. 100, 10 AP's
Artist-made paper

241 *Spiral* 1988
Mixed media, embossed
5 colors—shades of mauve, grey, black
25 x 36 (63.5 x 91 mm.)
Ed. 100, 10 AP's
Artist-made paper
Collection: Hewlett-Packard, VA;
Real Veal Inc., Ixonia, WI

242 *Red Planet* 1988
Mixed media, embossed
5 colors—pink, red, crimson, grey, blue
25 x 36 (63.5 x 91 mm.)
Ed. 100, 10 AP's
Artist-made paper
Color plate page 45

243   *North Range I & II* 1988
Mixed media, embossed
6 colors—mauve, pink, lt. yellow, grey, blue
25 x 72 (63.5 x 182 mm.)
Ed. 100, 10 AP's
Artist-made paper
Collection: Monsanto Co., Application
Development Center, Springfield, MA

244   *Solar Winds I & II* 1988
Mixed media, embossed
5 colors—lt. yellow, peach, grey, blue, pearlescent russet
25 x 72 (63.5 x 182 mm.)
Ed. 100, 10 AP's
Artist-made paper
Collection: Ruckert & Mielkle Enginering, Waukesha, WI
IBM Corp., Raleigh, NC

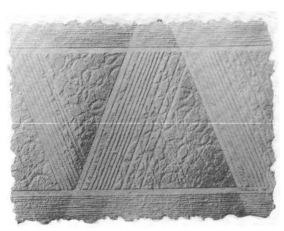

245   *Triad* 1988
Mixed media, embossed
4 colors—blue, mauve, pink, pearlescent white
25 x 36 (63.5 x 91 mm.)
Ed. 100, 10 AP's
Artist-made paper
Collection: Fayetteville Museum of Art, NC

246   *Greeting Card* 1988
Etching
2 colors—lt. blue, pink
6 x 4 (14 x 10 mm.)
Ed. 400
Artist-made paper

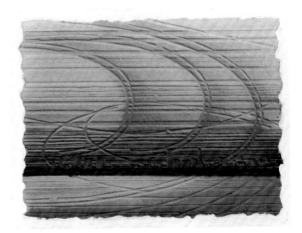

247   *City Island I & II* 1989
Mixed media, embossed
6 colors—tan, peach, grey, dk. blue, russet
25 x 72 (63.5 x 182 mm.)
Ed. 100, 10 AP's
Artist-made paper

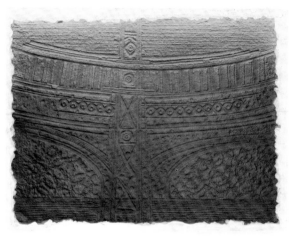

248 *Park View* 1989
Mixed media, embossed
4 colors—mauve, pink, turquoise, violet
25 x 36 (63.5 x 91 mm.)
Ed. 100, 10 AP's
Artist-made paper

249 *Lotus* 1989
Mixed media, embossed
5 colors—peach, pink, green, violet, blue
25 x 36 (63.5 x 91 mm.)
Ed. 100, 10 AP's
Artist-made paper

250 *Vines* 1988
Mixed media, embossed
2 colors—lt. green, dark green
25 x 36 (63.5 x 91 mm.)
Ed. 100, 10 AP's
Artist-made paper

251 *Quadrate* 1989
Mixed media, embossed
5 colors—blue, violet, red, yellow, silver
25 x 36 (63.5 x 91 mm.)
Ed. 100, 10 AP's
Artist-made paper

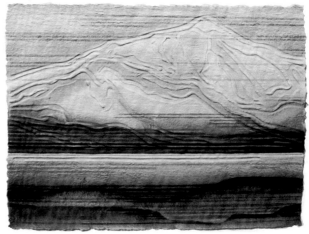

252 *Red Hills I, II, III, IV* 1988
Monoprints
8 colors—green, brown, rust, grey, green
36 x 192 (91 x 488 mm.)
1/1
Artist-made paper
Collection: Commissioned by Northern Telecom Inc., McLean, VA

253 *Sounding* 1989
Mixed media, embossed
6 colors—blue, black, mauve, cream, metallic
gold & pearlescent
25 x 36 (63.5 x 91 mm.)
Ed. 100, 10 AP's
Artist-made paper
Color reproduction on dust jacket

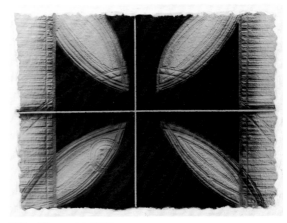

254 *Transept* 1989
Mixed media, embossed
4 colors—violet, black, greys
25 x 36 (63.5 x 91 mm.)
Ed. 100, 10 AP's
Artist-made paper

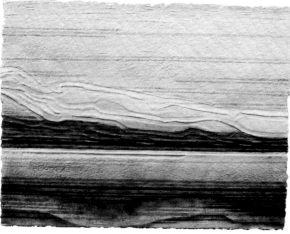

255 *Shield* 1989
Mixed media, embossed
6 colors—pink, mauve, green, blue
25 x 36 (63.5 x 91 mm.)
Ed. 100, 10 AP's
Artist-made paper

256 *Echo Fields* 1989
Mixed media, embossed
4 colors—green, grey, pink, maroon
25 x 36 (63.5 x 91 mm.)
Ed. 100, 10 AP's
Artist-made paper

257 *Triangle I, II* 1988
Monoprints (a total of six variations were created)
4 colors—pink, mauve, blue, pearlescent
25 x 36 (63.5 x 91 mm.)
1/1
Artist-made paper
Collection: Toshiba, NJ; Cooper & Lybrand, NJ

PERSONAL BIOGRAPHY

Marjorie Tomchuk

1933
Born in Fisher Branch, Manitoba, Canada.
Lived on a farm which her father homesteaded.
Youngest of three children; brother: Steve, sister: Jean.

1939-46
Attended elementary school in Fisher Branch.
The family moved briefly to Winnipeg, then returned to live in the town of Fisher Branch, later moved to a second farm location.

1947-49
Family moved to Winnipeg, Manitoba, while still maintaining their farm which was worked during the summer months.
Attended Mulvey Junior High School.

1949-1951
Attended Gordon Bell High School, Winnipeg.

1951-52
Employed at the Imperial Bank of Canada, Winnipeg.

1952-53
Entered the School of Interior Design, University of Manitoba.

1953
Moved with family to Michigan.
Attended the College of Architecture and Design, University of Michigan, Ann Arbor. Majored in graphic art and art education.

1957
Graduated from the University of Michigan with a Bachelor of Science in Design.

1957-58
Travelled and worked in four cities: San Francisco, Los Angeles, New Orleans, New York. Employed by commercial art studios.
Spent Christmas in Mexico City.

1959
Death of Mother.

1959-60
Returned to Michigan. Employed by the Lincoln Park Public Schools as an art teacher.

1960
3 months spent travelling: Scotland, England, France, Spain, Italy.

1960-61
Attended the University of Michigan, Horace H. Rackham School of Graduate Studies, earned a Degree of Master of Arts (Art).

1961
Moved to Long Beach, California. Employed by the Long Beach Public Schools as an art teacher. Enrolled at the Long Beach State College, Art Department to take evening classes in printmaking with Dick Swift.

1962-64
Lived in Tokyo, Japan. Worked as an art teacher with the American Dependent Schools. Took Saturday classes in woodblock printing from Toshi Yoshida and sumi-e lessons with Uchiyama. Enrolled in evening classes at the Sophia University to study Chinese and Japanese art history.

1963
Death of Father.

1963
Spent the year travelling throughout Japan. Summer travels included India, Kasimir, Nepal, Burma, Cambodia, Malaysia, Singapore and Vietnam.

1964-65
Moved to Frankfurt, Germany. Employed by the American Dependent Schools as an art teacher. Travelled to Germany by way of India, Egypt, Greece, Italy and Switzerland. Travels during vacations included Prague, Moscow, Leningrad, Oslo, Stockholm and Copenhagen.

1964-65
Spent weekends working on etchings at the studio of Helga Kaiser, Schönberg, Germany.

1965-68
Moved to New York City. Worked in the suburb of Spring Valley, NY as an art teacher.

1966
Enrolled in printmaking classes and participated in open workshops at Pratt Graphics Center, NYC. Studied etching with Michael Ponce de Leon.
Moved into an art studio located at 38 MacDougal St. NYC, (SOHO). Installed an etching press and began publishing print editions.

1967-68
Travels included trips to the Yucatan and Chichen Itza; Caracas, Venezuela; Trinidad and Eastern Canada.

1968
Ended teaching as a career, devoted time solely to art.
Began to sell editions of prints exclusively to Lublin Graphics Inc.

1970
Married Howard Aronson.

1970-74
Travels included trips to London, Holland, Italy, Hawaii, Mexico. Frequent trips to various U.S. cities produced a wealth of photographs from which the "Americana" series of etchings were produced.

1971
Moved from New York City to New Canaan, CT.
Became a member of the Silvermine Guild of Artists in New Canaan. Established a complete printmaking studio, and continued publishing editions.

1972-78
Elected to serve on the Board of Trustees, Silvermine Guild of Artists.

1974
Began "Motherhood" with son, Miles.

1976
Co-Chairman of the 11th National Print Exhibition, Silvermine Guild of Artists.

1976-89
Editions of prints were published and distributed exclusively by the artist. Participated in Art Expositions such as "Wash Art" and "Art Expo."
Association began with Sylvia Olejniczak, who acted as exhibition director.

1979-89
Travels with husband and son continued: Greece, Crete, Rhodes, Portugal, Kenya, Austria, Hawaii, Fiji, Japan, Australia.

1981-89
Extensive experimentation in artist-made paper led to a unique development of style, with the use of a textural paper quality and heavy embossing.

CHRONOLOGY OF ART CAREER

1962
Editions: 2 editions published by the artist

1963
Group Exhibition: National Print Exhibition,
  Ueno Museum, Tokyo, Japan
Editions: 1 edition published by the artist.

1964
Editions: 8 editions published by the artist

1965
Collection: Davison Art Center, Middletown, CT
Editions: 1 edition commissioned by John Barton
  Associates, NYC, NY
7 editions printed by the artist.

1966
Group Exhibition: National Print Exhibition,
  Potsdam, NY
Editions: 6 editions published by the artist

1967
Group Exhibition: 12th Biennial National Print
  Exhibition, Albany Print Club, Albany, NY
The Koltnow Gallery, NYC, NY
Collection: Davison Art Center, Middletown, CT
Editions: 12 editions published by the artist
2 partial editions commissioned by New York Graphic
  Society, Greenwich, CT

1968
Group Exhibition: Open Print Show, Providence Art Club,
  Providence, RI
The Koltnow Gallery, NYC, NY
Grippi Gallery, NYC, NY
Editions: 4 editions commissioned by Lublin Graphics,
  Inc., NYC, NY
2 editions commissioned by John Barton Associates, NYC,
  NY
2 editions published by the artist

1969
One-Woman Exhibition: Lyn Kottler Galleries, N.Y., NY
Editions: 7 editions commissioned by Lublin Graphics,
  Inc., NYC, NY
1 edition commissioned by John Barton Associates, NYC,
  NY
4 editions published by the artist.

1970
Group Exhibition: Art in Air and Space, Miami Art Center,
  Miami, FL
17th National Print Exhibition, The Brooklyn Museum,
  NY
National Print Exhibition, The Print Club, Philadelphia,
  PA
Collection: Museum of Native American Cultures, Spokane,
  WA
Editions: 8 editions commissioned by Lublin Graphics, Inc.
  Greenwich, CT
1 edition commissioned by Ferdinand Roten Gallery, Inc.,
  Baltimore, MD
8 editions published by the artist

1971
Group Exhibition: 4th International Miniature Print
  Exhibition, Pratt Graphics Center, NYC, NY
Boston Printmakers, 23rd Annual Exhibition, DeCordova
  Museum, Lincoln, MA
3rd Annual National Print Exhibition, Atlanta, GA
Collection: DeCordova Museum, Lincoln, MA
Award: DeCordova Museum Purchase Prize, Boston
  Printmakers Exhibition
Editions: 4 editions commissioned by Lublin Graphics,
  Inc., Greenwich, CT

1972
One-Woman Exhibition: U.S. Military Academy Library,
  West Point, NY
Group Exhibition: Audubon Artists 30th Annual
  Exhibition, NYC, NY
Photo-Graphics Workshop, New Canaan, CT
Prints and Drawings, Town Hall Art Gallery, Stamford, CT
National Arts Club, Drawing & Print Exhibition, NYC, NY
Award: National Arts Club Award
Editions: Commemorative Poster, 50th Anniversary,
  commissioned by Silvermine Guild of Artists, New
  Canaan, CT
1 edition commissioned by Lublin Graphics, Inc.,
  Greenwich, CT

1973
Group Exhibition: American Printmakers, F 15 Gallery,
  Moss, Norway
The Boston Printmakers 25th Exhibition, Lincoln, MA
23rd National Exhibition of Prints, Library of Congress and
  the National Collection of Fine Arts, Washington, DC
Lublin Graphics exhibition of Gallery Artists, Tokyo,
  Japan
Stamford Art Association Juried Exhibition, Stamford, CT
Collections: National Air & Space Museum, Smithsonian
  Institution, Wash. DC
DeCordova Museum, Lincoln, MA
Awards: DeCordova Museum Purchase Prize, Boston
  Printmakers Exhibition
1st Prize, Stamford Art Association
Editions: 3 editions commissioned by Lublin Graphics,
  Inc., Greenwich, CT

1974
One-Woman Exhibition: Art Barn Gallery, Greenwich, CT
Group Exhibition: 10th National Print Exhibition,
  Silvermine Guild of Artists, New Canaan, CT
Graphics Exhibition, Stamford Art Association, Stamford,
  CT
Collection: The Denver Art Museum
Editions: 4 editions commissioned by Lublin Graphics,
  Inc., Greenwich, CT
Partial edition commissioned by Original Print Collectors
  Group, NYC, NY

1975
One-Woman Exhibition: Gallery of Originals, Tacoma,
  WA
Group Exhibition: Silvermine Guild of Artists Print
  Members Exhibit, New Canaan, CT
United States Military Academy Library, West Point, NY
Collection: Midwest Museum of American Art, Elkart, IN
Editions: 3 editions published in part by Lublin Graphics
  and the artist

1976
One-Woman Exhibition: Silvermine Guild of Artists, New
  Canaan, CT
Group Exhibition: 11th National Print Biennial,
  Silve:mine Guild of Artists, New Canaan, CT
Collections: The Library of Congress, Washington, DC
Butler Institute of American Art, Youngstown, OH
Editions: 3 editions published by the artist

1977
One-Woman Exhibition: The Gallery, G. Fox & Co.,
  Hartford, CT
Wilton Gallery, Wilton, CT
Group Exhibition: Kerwin Galleries, Burlingame, CA
Collection: Nelson Gallery of Art, Kansas City, MO
Editions: 1 edition published by Original Print Collectors
  Group, NYC
4 editions published by the artist

1978

One-Woman Exhibition: Artworks at the Wayne, Providence, RI
The Lakeside Press, R.R. Donnelly & Sons Co., Chicago, IL
Washington International Art Fair, DC National Armory, Wash., DC, Leavenworth Public Library, Leavenworth, KS
Group Exhibition: La Gallerie, Hamden, CT
Editions: 4 editions published by the artist
1 poster published by the artist.

1979

One-Woman Exhibition: Horton's Gallery of Fine Art, Grand Rapids, MI
World Art Exposition, Hynes Auditorium, Boston, MA
International Art Exposition, New York Coliseum, NYC, NY
Washington International Art Fair, DC National Armory, Washington, DC
The Connecticut Gallery, Hartford Civic Center, Hartford, CT
Group Exhibition: The Greenwich Workshop, Fairfield, CT
Editions: 18 editions published by the artist
3 posters published by the artist

1980

One-Woman Exhibition: International Art Exposition, Coliseum, NYC, NY
Washington International Art Fair, DC National Armory, Washington, DC
Prints '80, International Meeting of Art Publishers, Los Angeles, CA
Art Expo West, Los Angeles Convention Center, CA
Group Exhibition: The October Gallery, St. Helena, CA
Wilson Art Center, The Harley School, Rochester, NY
Editions: 9 editions published by the artist
4 posters published by the artist.

1981

One-Woman Exhibition: Prints '81, International Meeting of Print Publishers, Los Angeles, CA
International Art Exposition, Coliseum, New York, NY
Washington International Art Fair, DC National Armory, Wash., DC
International Art Exposition CA, Showplace Square, San Francisco, CA
Group Exhibition: New Canaan Society For the Arts, The Carriage Barn, New Canaan, CT
Editions: 1 edition commissioned by Dartmouth Alumni, Class of '54
2 editions published by the artist
4 posters published by the artist

1982

One-Woman Exhibition: International Fine Arts Gallery, Ft. Lauderdale, FL
International Art Exposition NY, Coliseum, New York, NY
Editions: 8 editions published by the artist
1 poster published by the artist

1983

One-Woman Exhibition: International Art Exposition NY, Coliseum, NYC
Washington International Art Fair, Convention Center, Wash., DC
International Art Exposition, Texas, Market Hall, Dallas, TX
Group Exhibition: 14th National Print Exhibition, Silvermine Guild of Artists, New Canaan, CT
Collections: Museum of the City of New York, NYC, NY
Library of Congress, Poster Collection, Washington, DC
Editions: 2 editions commissioned by Art West Designs, Lakewood, CO
12 editions published by the artist
3 sculptured paper editions published by the artist
3 posters published by the artist

1984

One-Woman Exhibition: International Art Exposition NY, Coliseum, NYC
International Art Exposition, Texas, Market Hall, Dallas, TX
Group Exhibition: The Whitney Shop, New Canaan, CT
Editions: 12 editions published by the artist
6 cast paper editions published by the artist

1985

One-Woman Exhibition: International Art Exposition NY, Coliseum, NYC
International Art Exposition CAL, Los Angeles Convention Center, CA
Editions: 9 editions published by the artist

1986

One-Woman Exhibition: Isetan Fine Arts Salon, Tokyo, Japan
International Art Exposition NY, Javits Convention Center, NYC, NY
International Art Exposition CAL, Los Angeles Convention Center, CA
Art Expo Miami, Coconut Grove Convention Center, FL
Group Exhibition: 'Liberty' Silvermine Center for the Arts, New Canaan, CT also, John Szoke Gallery, NYC, NY
Editions: 1 edition commissioned by Isetan Gallery, Tokyo, Japan
4 editions published by the artist

1987

One-Woman Exhibition: Raleigh Contemporary Gallery, Raleigh, NC
International Art Exposition NY, Javits Convention Center, NYC, NY
Art Expo Miami, Coconut Grove Convention Center, FL
International Art Exposition CAL, Los Angeles Convention Center, CA
Group Exhibition: Women Printmakers, N.E. Missouri State University, Kirksville, MO
Award: Original cast paper, commissioned by Xerox Corp., Stamford, CT
Editions: 6 editions published by the artist

1988

One-Woman Exhibition: International Art Exposition NY, Javits Convention Center, NYC, NY
International Art Exposition CAL, Los Angeles Convention Center, CA
Group Exhibition: "Women Printmakers," Missouri Western State College
The Gallery, Barnegut Light, NJ
U.S. Paper Makers Workshop, color slide presentation, Finnish Artists Society, Summer University of Tampere
"Print Types" Kansas Union Gallery, Kansas State University, Manhattan, Kansas
Commission: "Red Hills," four panels of original art created for Northern Telecom, McLean, VA
Editions: 10 editions published by the artist

1989

One-Woman Exhibition: International Art Exposition NY, Javits Convention Center, NYC, NY
International Art Exposition CAL, Los Angeles Convention Center, LA
White Gallery, Franklin Lakes, NJ
Two-Women Exhibit: Fayetteville Art Museum, Fayetteville, NC
Group Exhibition: "Women Printmakers" Carleton College, MN and North Hennipen Community College, Minneapolis, MN
Collection: Fayetteville Art Museum, Fayetteville, NC
Editions: 8 editions published by the artist

CORPORATE COLLECTIONS (partial listing)

Allstate, FL; Allstate, Northbrook, IL
American Communications Inc., IL
American Standard Corp., NJ
Anheuser-Busch Inc., St. Louis, MO
Apple Computor, VA
Arundel Communications, IL
AT&T, Bell Labs, PA; AT&T Information Systems,
   Chicago IL
Bell Atlantic, Silver Spring, MD
Bell & Howell, IL
Blue Cross/ Blue Shield, VA
Charles Brand Co., NY, NY
Bunker Ramo, CT
Burlington Northern Railroad, IL
Burnup & Simms, FL
Cellularone, Detroit, MI
Citicorp, IL; Citicorp Mortgage Corp., Trevose, PA
Chancellor Capital Corp., TX
Connecticut Bank & Trust, Westport, CT
Continental Group, CT
Continental Webb, IL
Counsellor Realty, MN
Covia Corp., United Airlines, IL
Dow Jones Headquarters, NY, NY
E. I. DuPont, NJ
Emerson Electric, St. Louis, MO
Exxon Corp., New York, NY
Facciani & Co., Independence, MO
Federal Express, TN
Federal Home Loan Mortgage Corp., Washington, DC
Ferber Mining Corp., Vancouver, BC, Canada
First Exchange Bank, St. Louis, MO
First Family Mortgage, IL
First National Bank of Boston, Boston, MA
General Accident & Insurance, IL
General American Life Insurance Co., St. Louis, MO
General Electric, CT
The Hammond Clinic, IN
Hayle Mill, Kent, England
Hearst Publications, N.Y., NY
Hewlett-Packard Co., VA
IBM Corp., NY; CT; MD; NC

Iowa American Water Co., IA
Kantor, Shaw and Davidoff. N.Y., NY
Lagastee Insurance, IL
Marcus, Ollman, Konsmer, N.Y., NY
Marriott Corp., NY, VA
Monsanto Co., MA; MI
Morton Thiokal, Reading, PA
National Bank of Washington, Washington, DC
New Canaan Bank & Trust Co., New Canaan, CT
New England Bell, CT
Ontario Government Ministry of Energy, Toronto, Canada
Ontario Government, Service Dept. Branch, Toronto,
   Canada
O'Sullivan, Beauchamp, Kelly & Whipple, Port Huron, MI
Pacific Mutual, Fountain Valley, CA
Playtex International, CT
Professional Liability Underwriting Managers, MN
RAM Mortgage, NJ
Ramada Inn, WV
Risk Management, Grand Rapids, MI
Riverside Publishing, IL
Ruckert & Mielkle Engineering, WI
Edward Rubin Associates, Hartsdale, NY
Sabin, Bermant and Gould, N.Y., NY
Sears Communications, Arlington Heights, IL
Southwestern Bell
Tanabe USA Inc., NJ
T-Bar Corp., Wilton, CT
Technical Documentation Services, MN
Tennico, VA
Time Inc., Chicago, IL
Toshiba, NJ
United Industries, St. Louis, MO
United Monetary Group, TX
Vanguard Atlantic Ltd., NY
Veda Inc., Arlington, VA
Veteran's Administration, Chicago, IL
Western Electric. N. Y., NY
Wilkinson, Barkee, Knauer and Quinn, Washington, DC
Wintrup, Stimson, Putnam and Roberts, N. Y., NY
Wyatt Co., Washigton, DC
Xerox Corp., NY, CT

MUSEUM AND EDUCATIONAL COLLECTIONS

Library of Congress, Print Collection, Washington, DC
Library of Congress, Poster Collection, Washington, DC
National Air and Space Museum, Wasington, DC
Museum of the City of New York, NY
Newark Museum, Newark, NJ
DeCordova Museum, Lincoln, MA
Nelson Gallery of Art, Kansas City, MO
The Denver Art Museum, Denver, CO
Davison Art Center, Middletown, CT
Fayetteville Museum of Art, Fayetteville, NC
Midwest Museum of American Art, Elkart, IN
The Butler Institute of Art, Youngstown, OH
Museum of Native American Cultures, Spokane, WA
University Club of Chicago, Chicago, IL
The Print Consortium, St. Joseph, MO
New Canaan Library, New Canaan, CT
Rockefeller Social Science Building, Dartmouth
    College, NH

SELECTED BIBLIOGRAPHY

"M. Tomchuk Prints", *Journal of the Print World*, Fall
    1982
"The Artist M. Tomchuk" *Prints* magazine, July-August,
    1983
"The Making of an Etching," *Decor* Magazine, March, 1988
"Embossed Paper Designs" Eric Grow, *Modern Style*, 1985
Sunstorm Magazine, October, 1987
Ellen Kaplan, *Prints, A Collectors Guide*, 1983
New York Art Review, American References, 3rd edition,
    1988
Art Business News Magazine, Jan. 1987; Feb. 1988
Ukranian Weekly, June 5, 1983
"Class of '54" *Dartmouth Alumni Magazine*, Dec. 1981
New Canaan Advertiser, May 27 1976; Sept. 8, 1977
Original Print Collectors Group Newsletter, Autumn, 1973;
    Volume V, No. 4, 1977
"Colored Etchings" *Hartford Current*, July 10, 1977
American Review of Art & Science, Volume VI, No. 4, 1969

Additional Listings

American Artists, American References
Who's Who in American Art
American Printmakers
Artists USA
Who's Who in the Arts
International Who's Who of Art & Antiques
World's Who's Who of Women
Print World Directory
Artists in Print Directory
Collectors Art, Limited Edition Print Guide
ArtSearch
Encyclopedia of Living Artists in America